THE TYSON TAPES

JONATHAN RENDALL

SCREAM

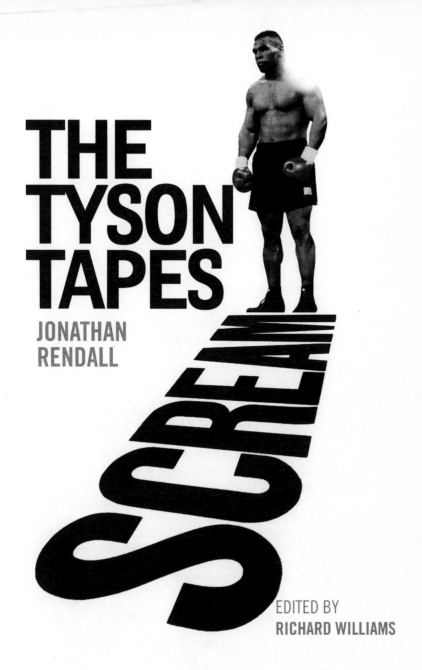

EDITED BY
RICHARD WILLIAMS

CB

First published in 2014 by Short Books
3A Exmouth House
Pine Street
EC1R 0JH

10 9 8 7 6 5 4 3 2 1

A CIP catalogue record for this book is available
from the British Library.

ISBN 978-1-78072-221-4

Printed and bound in Great Britain by CPI Group (UK) Ltd,
Croydon, CR0 4YY

Cover design by Two Associates

Contents

Contents

Foreword

No one of his generation wrote about boxing as beautifully as Jonathan Rendall, who could make his readers feel as though they were not just at ringside, whether at Madison Square Garden or a small hall in London's East End, but right there in the corner, cutting the tape from a fighter's fists or rinsing the blood off his gumshield. Rendall's death in January 2013, aged 48, provoked not just grief among his friends and former colleagues but a deep and widespread regret that so distinctive a voice had been prematurely stilled.

The silence had effectively descended several years earlier, when the career of this enormously gifted and attractive man finally fell victim to his own chronic unreliability. Stories of his reckless disregard for deadlines were told at his funeral; still carrying echoes of the amused exasperation with which his behaviour was once viewed by his colleagues, they nevertheless glowed with the unstinted admiration that his talent inspired.

In 1998 Rendall won the Somerset Maugham Award for young writers with his first book, *This Bloody Mary Is the Last Thing I Own*, a brilliantly entertaining account of his adventures in the world of prizefighting. Previous winners had included Doris Lessing, Kingsley and Martin Amis, Ted Hughes, V.S. Naipaul, John le Carré, Michael Frayn, Angela Carter, Ian McEwan and Julian Barnes. Rendall was in his early thirties, and there was every reason to believe that he might one day achieve serious literary stature. I was one of a succession of editors at the *Sunday Correspondent*, the *Independent on Sunday*, *The Times* and the *Observer* who had already learned to be wary of his attitude to newspaper deadlines, but a degree of unreliability was the price many were prepared to pay for writing of such remarkable quality. This was particularly true when he devoted his attention to boxing, a sport whose metabolism he tuned into with a rare acuteness and sensitivity.

There would be two further books. *Twelve Grand* was about gambling, another of his obsessions. *Garden Hopping* was about the search for his birth mother (he had been given for adoption in infancy). His next was to be a full-scale biography of Mike Tyson, whose own once-glittering career was then in the throes of a spectacular meltdown. Since Jonathan had covered his fights, including the one that took place in a Washington courtroom, where the former world heavyweight champion was accused of rape, and knew many of the participants in the sporting and personal drama, he seemed ideally placed for the task.

Life, however, got in the way, and the work was never completed, at least as first envisaged. Attempts to take a different approach to the subject were rejected by the original publisher, and for several years Amazon's vain promise of the book's imminent appearance was the only indication that the project had ever existed at all.

It took Jonathan's death to reveal, amid his scant surviving possessions, the existence of a manuscript, into which he had clearly put considerable effort but for which his hopes seemed to have been extinguished. When I was invited to read it, I was immediately convinced that, despite failing to meet the terms of the original commission, the author had ended up with something equally valuable in terms of the historical record – and, in its inventiveness, truer to his own talent.

Scream – the book's title since the beginning – now concentrates on two interleaved approaches to the story: the oral testimony of some of the people who were closest to Tyson in his early days, given in interviews with Rendall in the early 2000s, and the author's attempt to put himself inside Tyson's head as the former champion reflects on the principal landmarks of his rise and fall. It is a high-risk approach, but Rendall's years on the inside of boxing (even, for a while, as the manager of a featherweight champion,

Colin 'Sweet C' McMillan) gave him a striking degree of empathy not just with the fighter at the centre of the drama but with the subsidiary cast of trainers, managers, cronies and hangers-on – some of them, such as the boxer turned writer José Torres and the matchmaker Johnny Bos, no longer with us. Their observations, pungent and sometimes contradictory, create a portrait whose impact is out of all proportion to the book's modest dimensions.

By comparison with the scale of Tyson's autobiography, published in 2013, this is a chamber piece: one in which the individual voices can be clearly heard even when they overlap and conflict, making the narrative resound with the clash of competing interests. In the process Rendall reconstructs not just the story of how a juvenile delinquent from the Brooklyn housing projects became one of the most celebrated and ultimately notorious figures of modern sport, but also a broader depiction of a world in which dreams and corruption, courage and brutality, altruism and venality walked hand in hand: the world of Mike Tyson. And, for an all too brief season, the world of Jonathan Rendall.

– Richard Williams

SCREAM

Glossary of Terms

KO	Knockout
TKO	Technical Knockout
NC	No-contest
RTD	Boxer Retired
DQ	Disqualification
Decision	Judge's Decision
WBA	World Boxing Association
WBC	World Boxing Council
IBF	International Boxing Federation
IBC	International Boxing Council

Dramatis Personae

Interviews with:

TEDDY ATLAS	Tyson's amateur trainer
JOHNNY BOS	Tyson matchmaker
JAY BRIGHT	Catskill house resident and Tyson cornerman
CRAIG	Tyson's sparring partner in Catskill
NADIA HUJTYN	Tyson's gym-mate and trainer for Cus D'Amato
STEVE LOTT	Tyson's cornerman and press agent
DON MAJESKI	Leading New York fight figure
FRANK MALONEY	Manager of Lennox Lewis and Julius Francis
KEVIN ROONEY	Tyson's professional trainer
JOSÉ TORRES	Former light-heavyweight champion

'I could have knocked him out in the third. But I did it very slowly. I wanted him to remember it for a long time. When I was hitting him to the body, he was making noises, like a woman screaming.'

– Mike Tyson, after knocking out Tyrell Biggs in the
seventh round on October 16, 1987.

Michael Gerard Tyson grew up in almost indescribable poverty in the ghettoes of Brooklyn. His mother, Lorna, was an alcoholic. His father, Jimmy Kirkpatrick – whom Tyson didn't know – was a burly odd-job man and womaniser who some said also acted as a local pimp. Incarcerated in young offender institutions from the age of ten, Tyson did, however, discover that he had extraordinary physical power. Plucked from reform school by a former boxer, Bobby Stewart, Tyson was introduced to the maverick septuagenarian boxing trainer Cus D'Amato, who housed boxers in a remote mansion in the Catskill mountains. D'Amato had trained the then youngest ever heavyweight champion, Floyd Patterson, some thirty years before, when he became known for campaigning against Mafia influence in boxing. D'Amato's idiosyncratic methods were based on an intricate series of numbers, denoting each punch or defensive movement. The idea was to leave the boxer free of independent thought. D'Amato preferred his boxers to be as emotionally empty and suggestible as possible, so that they could be rebuilt from scratch. D'Amato also espoused an unusual view about money, saying that it was 'the type of stuff you throw off the back of trucks'. As is well known, Tyson's rise was meteoric, and his fall equally so. What follows is an oral history of the Tyson years, largely provided by those who knew him intimately from the beginning. Here, then, are the Tyson tapes.

Part One
THE HOUSE

March 1981

Mike Tyson sat in the passenger seat. Bobby Stewart was driving. Mr Stewart was the coach from Tryon. Mike was twelve. He knew he could easily pass for twenty. Sometimes he liked that, but mainly he didn't. He had his cheap athletic clothes on. But that was an improvement from the stuff he'd had to wear in Bed-Stuy and Brownsville. Sometimes he'd had to put cardboard in his shoes. That was bad. The memories were too bad. His mother hadn't once been in touch since he'd been in Tryon. She could have sent him a present. That could make him cry but you can't show weakness. The only good thing really was his sister, Denise. She played him up as a tough guy and he liked that. She said things like, 'My brother is never "Mike" or "Tyson". He is always "Mike Tyson".'

Bobby kept drilling him about how he should act when they got to the gym in this out-of-the-way place and met this old Italian guy, Cus, and these other guys. Be polite. Always call them 'sir'. But what was in it for Bobby? Maybe this was a con. They had already hatched a plan, which was for Bobby to tell Cus that Mike was less schooled at boxing than he was. Not that Mike was very schooled at all. But they had boxed quite a few rounds and Mike knew that he had pushed Bobby sometimes even though Bobby was twice his age and had been a professional light heavyweight and Mike hadn't boxed once before.

Mike liked Bobby, to an extent. He didn't know if he could trust him, though. For a start, Bobby was white. He'd probably had the things white kids had, like the latest comic books, without having to steal them. On the other hand, white kids probably hadn't done some of the funny things he had, like drinking brandy and beer and smoking cigarettes and reefers and holding some other kid's gun. Man, but did he like that beer! And he was a world expert on brandy. He knew every single brand. But his privileges at Tryon had certainly got much better since Bobby started teaching him boxing. Maybe Bobby was using him and he was using Bobby for a way out of Tryon. But, why shouldn't he? He didn't want to stay there forever.

Mike looked out of the car window at the Hudson river. It was amazing up here, so near to New York and so different. All the forests and the glistening water. It was like a magic kingdom. Crazy! But he didn't let on his excitement to Bobby. Then his thoughts went to Brownsville, to the wind billowing through the derelict buildings in winter, and the terrible smell of the trash in summer, and the view down to the, the... howling streets from the roof where he kept his pigeons. They'd probably all have been taken by now. He knew every bird. But he'd get them back if he ever got out. And kick some ass while he was doing it.

But most of all he thought about the fear. Denise didn't know about that. Being scared all the time. Every minute he was out there. Sometimes he'd hide inside the walls of the derelict buildings. Inside them! That was pretty crazy, too. And hiding there he'd be so scared he thought he'd die of it. Right there. People thought he was so much older than he was because of his size. It wasn't fair.

Sure, he'd kicked a few asses, but not nearly as many as Denise thought. She just liked hearing that he had. That wasn't really his thing, though sometimes you had to. He liked to think of himself as more of a thief. It was cool being accepted by the older kids in the Puma Boys and he knew they were OK about having him around because he was fast. He liked to think there wasn't a pocketbook or a wallet he couldn't get. Whoosh! Mostly they didn't even know it was gone. It wasn't getting them that was the problem, it was not getting caught by the cops when he was running away. They may have caught him a few times but they didn't know how many times they didn't! OK, maybe that was an exaggeration. But it was still cool to think about. Real-life cops and robbers. Maybe if he'd had more practice, and if there was a Top Ten of

Brooklyn pickpockets, he could have got into it eventually.

Mr Stewart said they were coming up to the turning. He said they'd probably spar three rounds. Well, if Mr Stewart was conning him, he could con Mr Stewart back. Easily. And he could con this old Italian guy, Cus, too. He knew he could. He could con anyone. They'd probably hate him, was the truth. They'd probably think he was nothing. At least he wasn't scared out here in the Magic Kingdom.

Mr Stewart was drilling him on a few more things but Mike was drowsy and wasn't listening any more. He eased back in the passenger seat, thinking about how he would get his pigeons back, and telling himself, it's a nice day out, anyway...

KEVIN ROONEY (Tyson's future pro trainer): Tyson was a street punk. Allegedly he did all these crimes, but I don't believe that happened. I believe he ran around with punks on the street and got arrested and they shipped him up to a boys' home. His mother and father weren't together and he was like stumbling through the streets of Brooklyn. He started getting a record at nine. At thirteen [sic] he goes up to Tryon. He asks Bobby to teach him to box and Bobby says, 'On one condition: that your attitude changes and your grades improve.' And just like that Tyson goes from being a failure to being an A student. So Bobby calls up Cus. Bobby was with Cus but he was from Albany, but he used to come down. Jimmy Jacobs and

Bill Cayton were managing him. And I sparred with Bobby and he could punch. So Bobby says, 'I've got this guy and you should check this guy out.' I was like 7 and 0 as a pro at the time. I was like the head honcho of the gym. So this is the day this kid Tyson is going to spar with Bobby Stewart and I thought I better check this out.

TEDDY ATLAS (Tyson's future amateur trainer): I understood where Tyson was coming from. That he was in prison, that he had nothing, that he would come running to us. It was an audition just to see what we saw. The teaching was going to begin after that. He wouldn't box again for months. We don't teach that way, trial and error. But we had to put him in that first day just to see if we wanted to buy.

JOHNNY BOS (future Tyson matchmaker): I thought he was a bad boy from the beginning, but they made him out to be a lot worse than he was. He was bad but no worse than a lot of people. Where I come from, everyone got arrested. He was a wannabe bad guy.

Mike looked out of the car window as they came into Catskill. It was amazing. It was like Toytown. All the little wooden houses. And the sidewalks, so... clean. It was all white people. He didn't see one brother about. They stopped outside a police station. The gym was upstairs. As he got out, a cop eyed him suspiciously.

Mike knew what he was thinking. He was thinking, 'What is he doing here?' They went round the back. Down some steps, then up some steps to the gym door. There was a tree to the right. Mike could feel some nerves starting in his stomach. Mr Stewart had said how important this was, and Mike hadn't taken much notice of that, but now he had to fight Mr Stewart. They walked in and Mike liked the old gym immediately. It was like Rocky, with old yellow boxing posters on the wall. His mother had never really taken him to church, but that is what it felt like, or even an ancient temple. Mr Stewart introduced him to the old guy, Cus, who was standing by the ring in old lumberjack clothes, and a young white guy called Teddy who had a scar down his face, and another young white guy called Kevin who Mr Stewart said was the star boxer of the gym. Mike mainly stared at the old wooden floor. He called them 'sir' and they told him to change. On the way to the changing room he noticed a heavy bag with numbers written all over it.

He and Mr Stewart only went two rounds but it was flat out. He really launched himself at Mr Stewart, and Mr Stewart hit back harder than he ever had at Tryon. In the second round Mike's nose started bleeding. He was glad that they didn't fight a third round like they normally did. He didn't think he'd done very well. Now they would think he was nothing. He got dressed and waited for Mr Stewart to come out. When he did, Mike said he bet this Cus said he was useless. 'No,' Bobby said. 'Cus said, "That's the heavyweight champion of the world".' But Mike didn't believe him. Why would anyone say that, after that? So it was a con, right? Well, maybe he could impress them in some other way...

KEVIN ROONEY: So Tyson comes in '81 and I watch him spar with Bobby Stewart. I was working over in Brookwood, which is a lock-down facility for juveniles. Lock-down. Tyson was up in Tryon, where he had a whole big place where he could walk in the outdoors or whatever. Where I worked the guys never saw outside unless it was the basketball in the summer. I was the recreation director. Bad boys... One kid killed his old man over dope and he was an addict. He's probably serving 25-to-life somewhere else now, but who knows. So I watch Tyson spar and the first thing I thought was that he was lying about his age because he looked eighteen and he said he was twelve. He looked older than that kid I had in Brookwood who'd killed his family. I mean he could have been twenty, twenty-one, but it turned out he was actually twelve. I thought he might be lying about his age to stay out of jail.

TEDDY ATLAS: The first day Bobby Stewart brought him for me to look at him, he was manipulative. He was twelve years old and 190lb so there was a force of nature there as far as his physicality. He was very raw, he didn't know much, but he was strong. Stewart was a twenty-seven-year-old former pro. He'd had fourteen pro fights, good amount of amateur fights, former AAU amateur light-heavyweight champion, and he had to open up just to keep Tyson from physically overpowering him. And Tyson goes two rounds and he got a bloody nose. There's an interesting thing about that. After we decided to train him, he didn't get a bloody nose for another two years. So if he was a 'natural', like people said, he wouldn't have got a bloody nose. When he was under our tutelage, he didn't get a bloody nose no more. So after the second round he comes back with this bloody nose and I take a towel and I wipe it and say, 'That's it.' I didn't want to see him get abused. I knew we were buying so I said, 'That's it.' I put some polish on his nose to stop the bleeding and I said, 'Get out.' Now the manipulation, the acting, comes in, because he needs to be sure we were going to buy. Now he starts, 'No! No! No! I'm going another!' This guy wanted me to believe that he wanted to continue. He was glad that I said stop. But he had to put that on because he had to be sure that the audition was passed. At that point I got right in his face in a very serious way and said, 'Maybe you didn't hear me the first time. Get out of the ring. I tell you what you're doing, not you.' And he got out.

Cus felt that even if it was an act, he had the capability to perform. He had the physicality to do it, and if we can harness that, if we can develop and nurture and supplement that, with that ability... The bottom line between acting and not acting is the doing it. You're doing it.

On the way up, Mr Stewart had told Mike about how this Cus had stood up to all the mobsters. This was back in the olden days, when the Mob ran boxing. And no one ever had stood up to them like Cus did. Not only did Cus make Floyd Patterson the youngest ever heavyweight champ, Mr Stewart said, but also by standing up to the Mob and being independent he made Floyd Patterson the most money of any heavyweight champ in history. And Mike was real, real lucky, Mr Stewart said. Because here he had a chance that few other boxers had ever had and could only dream of. Because if Mike played his cards right and performed well and did exactly what they said, he would have the chance of following in Floyd Patterson's footsteps. And this made Mike think, but not in the way Mr Stewart thought he would. Because it didn't add up. Like in Brownsville if you were a goody-goody like his brother Rodney then people like the Puma Boys might bully you a bit but basically they would leave you alone because you weren't on their patch. But Cus was on the Mob's patch with Floyd Patterson so why didn't they deal with him like the Puma Boys would? Maybe this Cus would be more difficult to con than Mike had first thought...

After the sparring he and Mr Stewart got back in the car and drove to Cus's house for lunch. They went up a main road – Highway 385, Mike noted; he was good with details like that – and then up a wooded track. Mr Stewart seemed pretty cool and knowledge-able about this area but to Mike it was still amazing.

And then they came round a bend in the track and there was this mansion. This great wooden house, with gardens and everything, rose bushes, sloping down to the Hudson river. They drew up by a tree and Mike asked Mr Stewart what type of tree it was. Mr Stewart said he didn't know, and he was probably wrong but he'd always called it a weeping willow. There was an old lady waiting for them. Her name was Camille. Mike didn't know whether she was Cus's wife or what. She seemed kindly and she paid special attention to him. He noticed that immediately. She took him into the kitchen for some lemonade. He was so excited. He couldn't help showing it. It was like a mansion from the movies. After what Mr Stewart had told him Cus had said, he felt better and more free than for a long while.

Cus arrived and sat him down. He talked to him for about an hour. Most of what Cus said he didn't understand, but that was only because he wasn't really listening. Mainly he just looked at Cus's face, trying to work out what was behind it and why the Mob had left him alone. Cus talked mainly about boxing but also about historical figures like Alexander the Great, who Mike had only dimly heard of. He just nodded and smiled his coy smile. Cus talked about fear, which got Mike's attention, but it didn't seem to be the fear he had experienced in Brownsville, and he drifted away and just nodded again.

The smell from the cooking that this Camille was doing was driving him crazy. It was so delicious. She really liked him, he could tell. She was really looking after him. After Cus had finished talking they went to eat. The white guy with the scar, Teddy, was there and so was the squat guy, Kevin, the star of the gym. There were chicken wings, bread and butter, corn. It was beautiful. At the end, outside, when Mr Stewart was getting the car, Mike asked Camille if he could pick a rose and take it back to show the boys at Tryon. He told her he'd never seen rose bushes and thought they were only for emperors and kings or very rich people. He meant it, in a way, but it was also a good thing to say. It would cement the way Camille felt about him and she would transmit it to Cus. Unfortunately the rose died on the way back to Tryon, but neither he nor Mr Stewart really gave a fuck. He knew he would be coming there.

STEVE LOTT (Tyson's future cornerman and press agent): To get some idea of how much control the Mob had back in the '40s and '50s you'd have to put fifteen Bob Arums and fifteen Don Kings together. Cus did his own fights, standing up to those guys. I mean, what he did was unbelievable back then.

KEVIN ROONEY: When Patterson got off the plane from the [1952] Olympics in Helsinki – and Floyd weighed 165lb then – Cus announced that this was the next heavyweight champion of the world. So Cus had this total vision, that Floyd was the one who was going to break this stranglehold that the Mob had on boxing.

DON MAJESKI (leading New York fight figure):
D'Amato was a very strange man. A genius. I met him a
few times. Very odd, paranoid, but a genius. D'Amato
was the first guy to realise that the live gate was subor-
dinate to the television. So when he had Patterson, he
was able to not deal with the Mob. Patterson was the
first boxer ever to make a million dollars. If you go
through the microfilm, you'll see every sports writer
deriding him as a cheese champion, a second-rate
fighter, and yet he's making more money than Rocky
Marciano, who's the greatest attraction since Dempsey
and Joe Louis. How? Because D'Amato knew how to
promote it to a million people. So in that sense he was
a genius.

Individually, he was a misogynist. He had all these
kids like Patterson coming from these orphan homes.
There has always been this rumour that he was homosexual. I remember years ago I was at a restaurant up
in East Harlem called Patsy's Pizzeria, an old relic
from fifty years ago. And there was an old boxing man
called Bill Daly who was around Carlos Ortiz and Lee
Savold and was a protégé of Jack Kearns. So I went in
there and in the corner of the place was a guy with a
big-brimmed hat, and Daly said, 'You see that guy?' I
said, 'Yeah.' And he said, 'That's the real manager of
Floyd Patterson.' I said, 'OK,' and it was this Fat Tony
Salerno. Now Salerno is the guy who moved upstate
to a summer home, which is why D'Amato moved
up there. Salerno apparently bought the house for
D'Amato – this is the rumour. In '59 and '60, Frank

Hogan, then district attorney in New York, came down on the Patterson–Johannson fight when he saw that Tony Salerno was the shadow promoter of the show. In any event the allegation was that Salerno put up the money for Patterson, that D'Amato was a front for him, and that's why D'Amato could afford to go in the face of the Mob and Frankie Carbo and all these guys, because he was protected by Salerno. He wasn't the great crusader people made him out to be, fighting against corruption, St George against the dragon. No. He just had his own Mob that protected him. And one of the examples is that Patterson had closed millions of dollars and yet D'Amato wound up really with nothing because they were raking all the dough. How did D'Amato wind up broke and bankrupt? Because really he was just a frontman. Because it was going to the Mob. But the fact is D'Amato was also a genius. A brilliant, brilliant guy, but crazy, that's the problem. Like this mad doctor, who went in there and concocted stuff and came out with Floyd Patterson. And then concocts up and comes out with Tyson. Tyson was a cunning guy. Maybe he sort of figured, 'How am I going to use them to my advantage?' I think that's what he was. He was a card. Like I said, everybody that D'Amato got, they came out of reformatories. Teddy Atlas was in a reformatory. Patterson. Tyson. Rooney, virtually. All these guys. So everybody there, there was something bent about them. So I guess Tyson walked in there and said, 'I con them, they con me, right? And how much can I use them?'

KEVIN ROONEY: It was '74 and I was living at the hospital that I worked in. They had a dormitory and I lived there. I was a housekeeper – mopping, doing the elevator. I had gotten into a fight with my father and I said to myself, 'I gotta get out of this house. I'm gonna kill him or he's gonna kill me, and one of us is gonna end up going to jail.' He was a drinker. He worked as a longshoreman. He had a good job but somehow fucked that up. I guess he was drinking too much. All of a sudden he stopped working. Then one time he started to push my mother around and I went after him. We fought and then he hit me right in the solar plexus and I was done. So the next time he pushes my mother around I hit him with a baseball bat. I was seventeen. So that's when I said, 'I gotta get out of here' – and I got that job at the hospital. I've been on my own since I was fifteen years old. My old man was a big drinker. Like we all can, he could be nasty. He was always saying shit.

I won the Golden Gloves when I was eighteen. I started fighting when I was sixteen. A gym opened up in the neighbourhood and I was a good athlete. Baseball, basketball – I wasn't tall but I could play. Me and Teddy were best friends growing up in Staten Island. We used to play basketball all the time. He lived up in an expensive house. I lived in a working-class neighbourhood. The working-class neighbourhood was at the bottom and Teddy was at the top of the hill. We were like thirteen, fourteen. He used to hang out with us. I used to hang out on the corner.

Heroin addicts, pill-poppers and drunks! That's how it was. And then he just started hanging out. I guess it was about '73. I did some things for about two years but then I thought, 'I gotta change my ways or something bad gonna happen.' That's when they opened that gym and I said, 'Let's go.' I was the only guy that stayed. All my other friends, they just gave up. After my junior year at high school I just quit school. Cus went through the eighth grade and then he quit school, too. Then he used to go to the library on Fifth Avenue. He would go in every day and read about history, read about this, read about that. Plus he was just different. Very smart. He was a genius. After I won the Golden Gloves, because there were other people coming around me, my friend Brian said, 'Talk to Cus D'Amato.' So I talked to him and Cus said, 'Come live here, free room and board. We'll set you chores around the house.' I mean I painted, mowed the lawn... Before, I went back to my job at the hospital and thought, 'Maybe I can get a year's leave of absence in case it doesn't work out.' But they said they couldn't do that. I was laying in my bed thinking, I don't want to be one of those guys hanging around the bars going, 'I could have been this, I could've been that.' So, I'm going. I came up here in '76. I quit the job and came up on the train.

Cus was sixty-six years old. He'd been retired. Cus was a very private person, very disciplined. About the Mob, he always used to say to me, 'Ignore them. As long as I ignore them, the mobsters, and don't recognise them in any shape or form, there's nothing they can do.' Because they were underground. And Cus came along with Patterson and refused to fight for Norris. He went out and got local promoters and Patterson was the first fighter to make a million dollars. But Cus had his own Mob up here, is the truth. Money was flown in. Legend has it Cus would give $5,000 to a bum on the street. Then later he opened the gym just to keep himself motivated, and hopefully someone would come out of that. And then… Tyson.

TEDDY ATLAS: It was a big day for Tyson. He's going to live in the house with us. He's on best behaviour. He's saying, 'Yes, sir.' And I remember – I was probably about twenty-two – saying to him, 'Stop with the "Yes, sir" crap because I know that ain't gonna keep up and you're gonna wanna say, "Fuck you," and you can't say that either.' So we're in the house having our first meal and Cus would overcook or get Camille to overcook and we had this big heavy table. And then you put the food on and there's probably a couple of hundred pounds of food. I'm exaggerating but Cus would go round and count how many chicken wings she was cooking and say, 'Listen, I eat five chicken wings so if everyone eats five that's thirty chicken wings' –'cause there was six of us – 'so you gotta make thirty.' And then if she didn't have thirty he'd go into the freezer to add to it. Cus had this thing about food, and that happens when you have too much time on your hands and you don't work for a living, and because – and I'm half joking – but all he did was sit around and I was in the gym training fighters all day. He wore his robe all day, he watched Barney Miller, that was one of his favourites, and the other was M*A*S*H, and then he'd get someone to drive him to the gym for a half-hour, maybe an hour, just to see what Teddy was doing with the fighters. And he'd say, 'Good job! Wow! These guys are really learning how to fight!' Then he'd go home. He wouldn't come with me because he said, 'Atlas will be there for five hours because he gets too involved with the kids. And I gotta get home because I gotta watch something else.' And to thaw whatever meat had to be thawed for the next day, in case he got caught short if he didn't. And that's the truth, but of course that's not what's written out there. That's not what Rooney will tell you, but that's the plain truth.

So Tyson's at the house on his first day, and I remember the cabinet was behind him and Camille is sitting there and I'm sitting over there, and there's Rooney and whoever, and we got all the food there, and Tyson is waiting and I'm peeking at him – because that was my business, and Cus said I had a talent for teaching, and to be a teacher you got to be able to see what really exists, behind the eyes, and I was trying to use it that day – and all of a sudden Camille says she wants serving spoons. There was only one serving spoon. So she says, 'Michael, get me a serving spoon.' Well, he jumps so fast, to please and be a good boy, that his leg gets stuck under one of the underpinnings. He picks up the whole table and everything starts sliding off the table. Camille's yelling, 'Oh my God!' because everything's gonna smash on the floor. And Tyson's going, 'Oh!' And meanwhile when he was knocking out these old ladies' teeth in Brooklyn he didn't show half that awareness of doing something wrong. Right there he was showing us again what he had to show us. He was contrite, he was concerned, he was sensitive, he was sorrowful. Now when you grow up in Brownsville and from the age of nine, ten, eleven you hide in the side walls of abandoned buildings to exist, and to hide from people, because you got guys chasing you or whatever, and blend into a wall, I would say you had the practice ground for blending into more walls when you got older.

So I'm looking at Tyson moving the table around as if he's moving a piece of melon around. I look at Cus and Cus goes, 'What power! The next heavyweight champion of the world! My God, look at that! What an animal!' He called him an animal, just spontaneously. The truth was now coming out. And I'm watching Tyson make out that he just killed a family. And I'm thinking, what a fucked-up place I'm in. Look at this shit.

STEVE LOTT: I don't care what Cus was. I care what he did. The only things he was interested in were his fighters. If you're a doctor and a patient comes in, and he's an absolute mess with all kinds of wounds, and two weeks later he's walking out in great health, you're a great doctor. So Cus sees this kid – Mike – and he knows he's bad, but that deep down that's not what he really wants to be. It's the junk that covers him from having lived in Brooklyn. And Cus knew that he couldn't take a whip to him – it was going to take time. Mike needed therapy to get out of the hole he was in, and Cus was the therapist. Mike came to that house as a fucking mess.

Mike was on the third floor, at the back. From his window he could see the Hudson and the woods of the Magic Kingdom. Kevin moved out of the room to make way for him. Kevin was sharing with Teddy. They were best friends from Staten Island or somewhere. Teddy wasn't as tough as he made out, but he was OK. Kevin was tough, and he was OK too. It was quite hard adjusting to the... whiteness of it all. All the chores they all had to do. Cleaning things up, mowing the lawn. He liked it, though! It was so different from Brownsville or Tryon or Spofford. But Mr Stewart had been right. It was such a chance. And here he was! Camille still liked him just as much. That was good.

Cus was very interested in him. He knew that he was interested in him only because of boxing, and that he was some project to Cus that he didn't fully understand, but that was OK, too. You couldn't ask for everything. The main thing was that he knew already that he was regarded as special. It didn't matter what the real reason was. And Cus was still taking him aside all the time and talking to him, and the thing was he was listening more, which was dangerous, because that's when they get you, and you get hurt. He would have to watch that. But basically he was so happy. When Denise phoned him, which Cus was fine about, it was like listening to a different world. His mother still never phoned him, though. It was like their world was spinning away.

And Cus introduced him to these other guys, Jimmy and Bill. They were going to be his managers when he turned professional. Bill was an old guy who was like some '50s businessman you would see in the movies. Very correct. Jimmy was more OK. He put his hand on Mike's shoulder. Maybe Bill thought Mike was special, too, but Jimmy showed it. Jimmy and Cus were close. They'd lived together in New York. Mike felt that there was a whole family enveloping him and it was all great. Mike loved the whole boxing thing, was the truth, all the history – Joe Gans, Battling Nelson – and he knew this surprised them. They hadn't bargained for that. He knew they thought he was basically an ape. And Jimmy had all these films. That was how he and Bill had made their money. Cus put a sheet up in Mike's bedroom so he could watch the films. He always said he would get a proper screen but he never did. Kevin and Teddy weren't really into the history of fights stuff. The only other one in the house who was, was Jay, the fat kid who didn't box and just helped Camille with the cooking. Both Jay's parents had died. But Jay knew the history stuff. Jay was obsessed by Muhammad

Ali. Cus asked for him to spar with Ali once. And Ali did it. Teddy took a film of it. And it was beautiful lying there watching these images of the old fighters burst onto the sheet in his bedroom like magic. Then the morning would come and Mike wasn't scared like in Brownsville.

Cus said the thing you had to think about each morning was when your opponent would be running. You had to run earlier than him. That's how you got an edge. So if you thought he ran at 7am then you would run at six. When they all ran together it would be two miles to the lights on Highway 385 and two miles back. The finishing post was the weeping willow. Often it was him and Kevin in a sprint. But sometimes Mike couldn't help his excitement and got up and ran alone at 4.30, because then no one could possibly be earlier, and there would be the smell of the dew and the fresh, wet leaves of the Magic Kingdom bouncing off his charging shoulders...

KEVIN ROONEY: For our roadwork, we went out of the house right on to 385. I was the best runner. I let Tyson beat me so he'd have confidence but every once in a while I'd show him who the real boss was. I could whip his ass but he was a good runner, a fast runner.

NADIA HUJTYN (Tyson's gym-mate and future trainer for Cus D'Amato): I was active in theatre at high school so I tried out for the play here, which was

A Streetcar Named Desire. And Kevin Rooney sat right next to me at the try-out. He was around twenty-two then. It was 1978. We started talking and then he got the lead. He was Stanley, I was Stella, and everything else went from there. All he ever talked about was: 'We can't rehearse today. I've gotta work out.' And when you're in the theatre you bond with people and become interested in what they do, and so I said I'd go to the gym, and I've been there ever since.

I found out long after the fact that it was very remarkable that Cus let me be there, because he didn't like girls in the gym, because no girls came for the right reason. But I came for the right reason. It was a while before I found a way to get there. Remember this was 1978. Girls did not box. I was living in Hudson. I drove to the gym, I ran, I rode a bike, whatever I had to do to get there, because that's how important it was to me. I was going to prove I was serious and I was going to do what it took to prove it. Foolishly, but I did.

The house was Camille's. It didn't have a name that I'm aware of but it was a seventeen-room Victorian mansion with ten acres. It was magnificent. Anyway, what I thought was, this is what I've always been looking for. Because of Cus, because of what I could feel, what I could see – what the fighters did. It was serious, dedicated and hard-working, very purposeful and directed. But it was a family. You knew that and felt that, too. And Cus was very protective of anybody that became part of the family.

I loved Cus. Cus was wonderful. I didn't want to just ask to train because not only was I just a girl, I was also a lot heavier than I am now and not necessarily athletic, so I had nothing to sell. When Cus said he was willing to teach me, I thought it was a gift. I'm not so sure any more but that's how I ended up there. Then, Kevin was pretty much the main man. But then Mike came. Just like they say, he came at twelve, and Bobby Stewart brought him. That day that they brought him I was there. And he was twelve years old and we all said to Cus, 'He can't be that age,' and Cus said, 'Well, I don't know. This man [Bobby Stewart] is my friend, so if he says he is then he must be.' And Mike was… he didn't know how to act with people. That was one of the things that he never learned. He didn't have any social skills. He didn't know how to behave. But he was all right with us in the gym. As time went on, he was fine.

But Mike wasn't brought up properly. Even Camille would say he had nothing. He didn't know how to act. He didn't know nothing. He didn't know about deodorants, he didn't know how to take care of himself. He didn't know about… nothing. Nothing. And here is this twelve-year-old, 185lb, with no refinement whatsoever. Things that you learn growing up in the home, he didn't learn those things. I mean he said to me one time, 'I figured out what to do! I figured out what you do.' And I said, 'What do you mean?' And he said, 'The girls at the dances. I figured out what you do. What you do is go and grab them by the hand

and you pull them out on the dancefloor really quick and then they can't say no and they have to stay out there with you till the song is done.'

TEDDY ATLAS: There was an incident when Tyson wouldn't bathe. He was very dirty. After I'd work him out hard, he'd really sweat. He would go upstairs and instead of showering he would throw cologne on himself. I got angry and told him to take a shower. We were downstairs one day and he took his sneakers off and you had to leave the room. Everyone in the room had to leave. It was so bad that Camille had to take the seat covers off the couch and wash them. One day we came home from the gym and he had been breaking out in his face with this disease. I didn't even understand what it was, but the doctor said there should be no cases of it, it was from the days when people didn't have no running sewers and you didn't have basic hygiene abilities. He had this. I had just come home from the gym and was putting my stuff away when all of a sudden Camille came down the steps and she was hiding, it looked like. And she was crying. She said, 'Don't say nothing to Cus.' She was really crying. I said, 'What's the matter?' She said, 'I just told Mike he smelled and to wash, and he said, "Fuck you, you piece of shit."' So I started going upstairs and started going after him and then Cus must have known something was going on because he came out to investigate and I'm halfway up the stairs and he goes, 'What's going on?' And I repeated what Tyson said and Cus said, 'Don't do nothing. I'll take care of it.' That was just one of many incidents.

KEVIN ROONEY: That's bullshit. I never heard before that Tyson called Camille that. And Atlas says Cus is in his robe and just watching TV? Get the fuck out of here. That's total bullshit. Atlas is just spinning it. Cus had no interest in TV. He would watch the news now and then but he had no interest. Atlas is trying to turn the whole thing around. Instead of paying tribute to Cus, he's stabbing him in the back. He's always been that way. The truth is the house was almost like the military. 'Cause Cus was in the military in the '40s but they never shipped him out to Europe. And he wanted to go there. He wanted to kill people. But he was an MP [military police]. That's what Cus's coaching was all about: discipline. And Tyson immediately accepted it. Bobby Stewart started it, I suppose. I can remember when Tyson was a kid, fourteen or fifteen, standing in front of the mirror and just practising, maybe throwing an uppercut or a hook, where everything turns at the same time. Tyson had power and he was bursting with speed. In my opinion he was the fastest ever. Faster even than Ali or Patterson.

Mike was sixteen. He had the same room and the same sheet for the old fights. In fact he'd taken over the chore in the house from Jay, of splicing the films on the projector. He'd started with 'smokers' – they were semi-legal fights, basically. Mainly they were kids but sometimes they were grown men. Then he had some proper amateur fights. He'd won the Junior Olympics two times. He liked to intimidate the other kids. He could do that, he'd found out. It was easy, though it wasn't really him. But it was still a tool. The other thing was that he'd got scared at the last Junior Olympics. It wouldn't have mattered but some fucking documentary crew had filmed it. He was crying on Teddy's chest. This white kid in the final didn't seem scared of him. He was just scared himself beforehand for a short while and they had caught it on film.

But the real problem was that he hadn't gotten to the actual Olympics. He knew that was part of Cus's project and it hadn't happened. But there was this other kid, Tillman, who just scampered about, jabbing him, in the Olympic trials. Tillman beat him two times. And then he'd been named a reserve for the Olympic team, and Cus had come up with this mad plan, about the super heavyweight, Tyrell Biggs, And the plan was to knock Biggs out in sparring so that they would have to suspend Biggs for medical reasons and that he would take Biggs' place. But that didn't happen. Instead they saw him trying to knock out Biggs in sparring, when he was supposed to be helping him to prepare for the Olympics, and they rumbled him and stopped it after a couple of rounds and sent him home. He didn't like Biggs. Biggs thought he was the big I-am of the team. As well, they had an argument over who was on the pool table and Mike had stormed to his room. So here he was, back home listening to the crickets in the garden at the house instead of being in Los Angeles with the team. But it was still 'home'. That shouldn't be forgotten. He was still 'up' overall.

First his mom had died and then his sister Denise had died, which was a surprise, almost unbeliev-able actually. But, being truthful, though he had been very sad, all that was ancient history now, as ancient as the old stories Cus told him in the kitchen about leaders from history. Neither his mom nor Denise had ever come to Catskill. Jimmy and Bill were around more, also José. José Torres, Cus's next champion after Patterson, at light heavy. The carrier of the torch of the peek-a-boo style! Just like him now! But Jim and Bill came to the house quite a lot these days, Jim more than Bill. Cus was closer to Jimmy than to José. He'd noticed that. Even though José had been his champion. But José was still part of the 'family'. Very much so. And José was now a writer. How do you figure that out, from a fighter to a writer?! But he liked this artistic dimension to the whole thing. It was cool. He understood it, which probably had surprised them too. Hello apeman! And Jimmy had a thing where when he met Mike he always kissed him. Mike liked that, too. So 'not Brownsville'. If you did that in Brownsville, you'd get shot. Teddy was not really responsive to the kissing type of thing. Nor was Cus, really, for that matter. Certainly not Bill. Bill just 'ran the business'. That's what everyone said. But yeah, Jimmy Jacobs. Thinking about it, he was this enigmatic, glamorous figure. He must have had a lot of money. Everyone said he did. He was like the Great Gatsby. He must have been a supreme businessman, but he didn't seem like a shark or a gangster. And in addition he had been world handball champion! The best ever! The Ali of handball! Jesus, unbelievable.

Mike listened to the crickets in the garden. Yes, he must make sure to stay in with Jimmy Jacobs, come what may. Anyway, Bill and Jimmy were thinking of turning him pro early, now that he hadn't gotten to the Olympics.

JOSÉ TORRES (former light-heavyweight champion): I met Mike back when he was about twelve. I became very interested in him because his manager was my manager. When Cus told me that this kid would become champion and he explained why, it wasn't so surprising. Because Cus was a very complex guy and I expected a very convoluted explanation. He explained that when he found out that Tyson used to get on public buses and wait until the people were warned about pickpockets before he would pickpocket them, he knew that he could transfer that into the ring and that it would be easy for Tyson because he was a very intelligent kid. And that was enough for me. I understood Cus and I knew Cus well. He was always talking about deceiving and lying because that's what you do in the ring. You deceive. And then when I saw Tyson training I thought, 'Now that's a great boy.' He was very strong, short, but I always believed that strength is not important. It's how you apply it. He was strong and fast but also smart, and I knew he would go places.

JAY BRIGHT (an orphan who was taken into the Catskill house at the behest of Jimmy Jacobs, and later became a Tyson cornerman): The highlight of my life was to spar with Ali. I have a videotape. Teddy drove. Cus went, and Kevin was there, too. Teddy actually taped it. It was special. I loved Ali when I was a kid. He was my idol. It was at his training camp at Deer Lake. The fighters' names are printed on the rocks. Ali's father did that, actually. Like Jack Johnson and all the famous fighters' names on the rocks. I think Ali gave it to a shelter or something. He gave the whole camp away. It's a beautiful camp. When we drove up, Ali was over the hillside – he was chopping wood. And we just sat and watched him chopping wood with an axe. It was part of his training.

Jimmy got me a tape of the second Frazier fight. That's when we became friends. I was in my early teens. I had gone to see an Ali exhibition fight in White Plains, New York. Me and my dad went up there, and we watched Ali fight an exhibition in like a community centre. And I came back and I wanted a tape of it. I'd become friends just before that with a guy who was Jimmy Jacobs' handball partner. He owned Ring Classics, which was on 8mm. This was before everybody had video machines. So I called him up and he said there's only one person in the world that would have a copy of the exhibition and that's Jimmy Jacobs. Jimmy was renowned as one of the best handball players ever. He also almost got in the US Olympic basketball team. And he was an expert shooter, too. He used to go around and give expert exhibitions to the New York police department on shooting.

So my friend gave me his number and I went down to Jimmy's office and I watched. He actually had a tape of the exhibition. 16mm. And he said, 'Would you like to see anything else?' And he showed me a film of Jack Johnson. Actually Jimmy was nominated for an Academy Award for best documentary about Jack Johnson. Then I started watching Joe Louis, Stanley Ketchel. I think I watched all of Ali's fights there. Jimmy had a projection room in his office. What happened was, at the weekend he would come down there and catch up with the work that he hadn't finished during the week. So he would be up in the office doing his work and I would sit there in the projection room. I loved it. I watched fight after fight. I was like a sponge.

JOSÉ TORRES: Ali punched from up here, from the shoulders. He never punched to the body. I killed people with body punches. I boxed with Ali in '71, in a gym in Miami two years before I quit. He said, 'Man, you are fast.' He was in his prime. When I saw a film of Jack Johnson, I was in shock. How similar Ali was to him. Ali said to me his style was based on

Jack Johnson. Not only his physicality, with his hands down, but his manner. Johnson talked to guys just like Ali. So, Johnson was first. With peek-a-boo, the idea is always to fight with your hands up. They throw punches and they can't hit me. It discourages them and they stop throwing punches. With Ali, when we boxed those two rounds in Miami, he couldn't hit me with the jab. But he was not only fast, he was strong and smart, and I was concentrating on defence. Ali was the most imperfect physical and the most perfect mental fighter. But, I tell you, Tyson would have been a dangerous fight for Ali. Tyson was a smart, fast puncher. But, if I had to bet, I would have bet on Ali.

DON MAJESKI: I think Rooney was closer. Teddy was an interesting kind of guy. Maybe his ego gets in the way. Maybe he thinks his opinion is more important than it is. What he says has to be the gospel, whereas Rooney's a more affable kind of guy. Atlas is an interesting case study. He tries to be a very cerebral kind of guy. Whether he is or isn't, I don't know. He feels that whatever he said is profound because he said it. A guy like Rooney doesn't attempt to be that way. He doesn't aspire to be anything except what he is. He's giving you a more truthful evaluation than Teddy, who thinks everything he's got to say has to be written in granite and set in stone for the next thousand years. So I don't know whether much of what Teddy says is what he believes or what he thinks you should believe that he believes. And the Lost Boys is a good analogy about those boys up there, because you're talking about a Peter Pan situation.

So, anyway, the business is that Cayton hooked up with Jimmy Jacobs, who himself had a curious background. A very arrogant, aloof kind of guy. Tyson had a cryptic thing he used to say: 'There are many strange things about Jim Jacobs that may never be known.' Jacobs would look at you as if, 'I am Jim Jacobs.' He and Cayton, they looked down on everybody. Cayton was like a prickly kind of guy. He was so awful. Jacobs was more gregarious. There was always the myth that Jacobs had great wealth, multi-millions, the wealthiest man in boxing. Cayton early in his career was in an advertising company and he got involved with the Friday night fights, finding the advertising. He got involved with Panasonic. And Jacobs came to him. He collected fight films. And Cayton saw this young guy who was gregarious and an enthusiast. And as it continued he would tend to let Jacobs go up front as the world's greatest authority on boxing and fight films. And Jacobs had accumulated most of them doing deals with the Mob.

At that early point in boxing – late '40s – there was no value to boxing films. There was no TV. They bought them for nothing and made millions. Dempsey, Louis, Jack Johnson, all these fights. So, for whatever reason, Cayton allowed Jacobs to be the front guy. Jimmy started getting these awards, getting in the Hall of Fame, and Cayton was happy to make the money. His ego never manifested itself until he started to get these fighters – Rosario, Tyson – and he says, 'I'm not getting any recognition. I'm not getting any of this and I should get more.'

So Cayton felt some resentment and his ego manifested itself, that 'I was the guy behind everything', that Jacobs was only the frontman. And yet Jacobs continued to put up this front. Like he was the wealthy guy, like he was the brains behind the operation, like he was financing Cayton. And it was completely the opposite. So he was a tremendous fraud – a great hoax that they perpetrated on the public. Amazing.

KEVIN ROONEY: Me and Mike were like brothers, and Jimmy was the guy he looked up to and Bill was like the brains behind the whole operation. Bill was brilliant. Mike was closer to Jimmy. Jimmy came from Cus. Bill, trust me, was the brains. He was gonna make Tyson the richest heavyweight in history. And then there was Cus. Despite what anybody says, I am not stupid. In '75, '76, I realised about Cus, this guy is very, very intelligent. I was nineteen years old, he's sixty-seven years old, but I would never have wanted to fight him. I mean his brother, Gerry, who got killed by a city cop... Once Gerry was coming home from work and one of the neighbours was getting the shit kicked out of him by seven guys who were all pounding on him, and Gerry waded straight into it and knocked out six people with seven punches. The other guy ran away. Cus was a teacher. Whatever he had to say made sense.

TEDDY ATLAS: And there were other times. I remember at the Junior Olympics, the first time I took Mike to fight in the Nationals in Denver. I'm responsible for everything. So at 7am we show up for the first day. It's a gymnasium that's just overflowing with fighters. It's like a cattle market. And there's tension. It's in the air. Because they're not there to pick fruit and vegetables. They're there to fight.

They're looking to see who could be their potential match. And here I am with Tyson, his big-time debut, really. He'd had about twenty fights. I'd been taking him to the Bronx and getting him fights. I'd developed him. And here's his first tournament. I got Mike standing there and already I see it going. He's using it already. He's fourteen years old and he's 210lb solid. He looks anything but a fourteen-year-old kid. Nothing but muscle. The others all look fourteen years old. They got acne. There's no muscle tone. And he's staring at them. He's just putting on this look that was gonna take advantage of what he knew was already going on in their minds. An imagination that could really destroy these kids. That they're thinking that he's older than he was, that he's a ringer, anything but a fourteen-year-old.

He is doing everything to let this thought process grow. To let this become real and start destroying these kids. When people ask him something, he doesn't answer. And I realise right away. I think, 'He's not a soldier. He's the Trojan horse. He's the guy who knows how to sneak into these guys' consciousness, and knows how to completely strip them of any chance they could have of performing.' He instinctively understood. I encouraged him by never discouraging him. Because he never knew that I knew what he was. And by not talking about it, by not saying you're bullshitting these guys or whatever, that was his go-ahead sign. You know, take them apart before they've even got a glove touched on them. It was: 'I'm just here to destroy people. I'm not here to talk. I'm not here to allow myself the follies that you humans allow yourselves. I'm just here to eat somebody. I'm just here to punch. Anything else, my guy here will give you anything you need.'

And when I didn't in any way reprimand him, he just saw that as, 'Let's go. Let's keep it going.' I knew what he was doing and, yeah, it was for my purpose, too. I could hear the bantering start. It was the first morning. And if I heard it, he heard it. I heard them saying, 'No, he can't be in this tournament.' And then the heavyweights, the guys he's gonna fight, 'No, there's no way. There's no freaking way.' Like one of the weaker ones would come over and say, 'My name's Bob.' Again, Tyson would just stare right through him. Right then I said, 'That kid will never get in the ring with him.' We got a lot of pull-outs. He knew exactly what he could do at that point. Sure enough, by the second day, we would get bussed by vans, and you had to be on the vans sometimes with potential opponents, and at the back of the bus I could hear them saying what they had come up with, about who he was. 'He's Sonny Liston's nephew.' From that point it got taken up. He was Sonny Liston's nephew. And he heard it and he never told anyone, 'No.' He knew this was good.

I think it was about the third day of the tournament. He'd knocked out a couple of guys. Then the tournament directors give you a day off and they take you on a tour, all the kids. To Pike's Peak. And it's way up and you get this tram and go up the mountain. And there's this time when you're waiting for the tram to come and all the kids are talking to each other and friendships are formed. Again Tyson is keeping himself just with me, not with anyone else. So there's these two kids in the heavyweight division and one of them says, 'What are you talking about? You got knocked out yesterday.' And the other kid goes, 'I'm smarter than you. You're a freaking dope. Look what you gotta fight. You gotta fight that.' They didn't even call him a name. They said that. As for that thing in the documentary where he's crying on me, that's just developing a fighter. He needed me. There was affection but there was also necessity – he was scared and it was before a fight.

KEVIN ROONEY: Teddy Atlas has nothing really to do with Tyson. Tyson came to Cus's house at twelve years old. Cus was breaking Teddy in to be a trainer. Atlas says he was Tyson's first trainer. He was not his first trainer. Cus D'Amato was his trainer, so let's get this right. Atlas worked Tyson's corner in his amateur fights and then he blew off in '82. That video shows Teddy doing something more than he really did. When I was boxing, Cus came to me and said, 'Rooney, I'm never going to work your corner. Teddy's gonna be your cornerman.' And I thought, 'OK, that's cool.' Teddy was my friend. But then Tyson enters the picture and Teddy gets jealous, I guess. Jealous of the attention that Tyson was getting, because Cus put up a big banner in Main Street in Catskill, when Tyson won the second national amateur championship.

The things that Teddy says, they're so far out I wouldn't even use them. To me it's bullshit. It's him talking. You know, Mike would confide in Cus, like, 'I'm ugly. Nobody wants me.' And Cus would say, 'When you become champion, you're going to have to fight the women off you.' Tyson did his bit with the chores, cleaning something up or something... Mike was very quiet at first. Here's a black kid from the ghetto in this big-assed mansion with all white people. So everyone was saying to him, 'Hey, Mike, what's up? How you doing?' I think he was comfortable but also the whole situation blew his mind. And anything reasonable that Atlas says is Cus D'Amato talking. He's trying to turn the whole thing around like he invented it. If he stood up and said, 'This is what I learned from Cus,' that would be better. That he's pretending that he invented it is what pisses me off.

NADIA HUJTYN: These days, Kevin doesn't say it

right. He doesn't say, 'Cus didn't say, "There's the next heavyweight champion of the world."' 'Cause Cus was no fool. He thought Mike could be heavyweight champ someday. He saw it, and barring any unforeseen circumstances he could be champion. Now what those unforeseen circumstances could be... It could be the young man loses desire. And if he loses desire, it doesn't make any difference about the rest.

And Teddy was a headcase even back then. You have to put up with this great respect for this individual. I know this individual. I know what he did to me. I know what he did to Cus. I know what he did to Kevin. As much as I don't approve of Kevin's behaviour now, the only reason Teddy was here, the only reason that he has the job he has now, is because he was Kevin Rooney's best friend. And he was in Rikers Island [penitentiary]. He was there for armed robbery. And Kevin begged Cus – 'cause they were having this programme where they would release these young men, rehabilitate them and all this – he begged Cus to intervene and get Teddy up here, so that Teddy could fight and train at the gym. So Cus did that, because of Kevin. Teddy had such a bad back that he wasn't able to continue to fight. So Cus said, 'Well, let me teach him to work with the young children.' He seemed to like to be with the young children, y'know – eight, nine, ten, twelve. Cus took on the responsibility of giving Teddy something to do. Cus was very responsible that way. He didn't necessarily like the things that Teddy did. And then Teddy decided he knew more than Cus, which was absolutely absurd. 'Cause here was a person who was not rational. Teddy is the same age I am. Forty-nine. We're all the same age. I look better than those two, I hope.

Anyway as far as Mike... Mike is a child. He wants a whole life that he never had. He tried to find a way to recreate it, but you can't. And that's what he wanted. He wanted a mother and father and the right home life. Mike often used to sleep in the living room on the couch, not in his room. I remember lots of times going over to watch the fights and he'd say, 'Would you tuck me in before you go?' That's where he slept, the back of the couch. Very child-like. Nobody gets that. That's what he is. It's like you kiss him and send him out to play. He would touch you constantly. It's like you'd pet a dog when you walked past. That's what he was like. Every time he walked by, he wanted this contact. I don't think it was a bad thing. I think it was because he never had it as a child and he was desperate for it. Desperate.

1984. Teddy Atlas is asked to leave the Catskill house by D'Amato after holding a gun to Tyson's head. Atlas believes Tyson has behaved lewdly towards his pre-pubescent niece. Tyson is returned briefly to Tryon. According to Atlas, Tyson was running scared and he is returned there for his own safety. Kevin Rooney takes over Atlas's training responsibilities as Tyson, having failed to make the Olympics, prepares to turn professional.

JAY BRIGHT: I used to go up there for the summers and stuff beforehand. My mother had passed away and I would go up there for the summers and my father would come and pick me up. Once Jim had made the introduction between me and Cus, he was my friend. We were all three friends. Then my father passed away, and then my brother passed away, and Cus asked me if I'd like to live up there and I started going to school up there. 'Cause I really didn't want to go back to New York City.

Cus had a whole bunch of Jimmy's fights up there and Mike's job later on when I was at college was the films. And my job before Mike came along was the films. They were 16mm, and they'd got kind of ratty. And Cus had a splicer that Jimmy had sent him, so one of my jobs, years before Mike took over the job, was to go through the films and watch for when it broke. You had to learn how to thread the thing. It wasn't like the newer ones where you just feed them into a hole. You had to get the pieces together and glue it together and splice it, basically.

Certain nights everyone would just sit around and watch the fights. We had a sheet and then Cus eventually got a projection screen, too – not big, like a plasticky kind of cloth, like a window shade. Oh, yeah, I trusted Cus's opinion about Mike becoming a future heavyweight champ, more than anything. If Cus said something like that, I wouldn't question it, never. It was something that was... fact. Cus wasn't wrong about boxing very often.

Something terrible had happened. Mike was back in a cell in Tryon. He couldn't really take it in, that it had happened at all and that he was now in this cell again. Surely this must be some kind of joke. OK, he had done wrong, but only marginally. It was only meant to be a joke, really. He'd pinched the ass of a relative of Teddy's, a little girl. Then he'd said something about how she might grow up real nice. She must have taken it wrong. And maybe he was slightly out of line, but he didn't mean nothing. Then the next thing he knows, he goes to the gym for his workout and Teddy turns up.

He didn't think nothing of it, until he saw how mad Teddy was. But Teddy didn't scare him. Teddy was a fake bad-ass. He wouldn't last one minute acting like that down in Brownsville or Bed-Stuy. If it wasn't for his scar, no one would be scared of him at all. But then Teddy surprised him. He pulled this gun out and held it to Mike's head. They were outside the gym at the back, by the tree. Even then Mike wasn't scared. He knew Teddy wouldn't kill him. Then Teddy pulls the trigger and blows a shot up into the air through the tree, as if it's a big bad-ass thing to do. He was acting like in some movie. And then Mike just ran off. He was pretty angry, though. And after he told Cus, Cus just basically bundled him down to this cell in Tryon through Bobby Stewart and told him Teddy would be gone from the house.

TEDDY ATLAS: I left Mike because of certain things.

When I call people on certain things it's not because I'm some perfect guy – far from it – but I feel I've got to hold myself accountable. I'm not going to say that when I left Tyson I understood everything there was to know, but I did feel that there was a substantial lacking in his person. Cus thought I left after I put the gun to Tyson but I was still around. What happened was I had gotten involved with a kid up there, whose brother used to come to the gym. And when I left, all the kids wanted me to continue training them. But I wouldn't do that because it just wouldn't be right.

Cus thought I had gone back to New York, and I was still there. And during this period I see Mickey Duff from England, who was close to Jimmy, not Cus, and he said it was a shame what happened with me, blah, blah, blah, but he just had to tell me something. I had to believe what he was telling me because there was no agenda there. And he tells me the whole plan at the Olympics about trying to knock out Biggs. And he said Cus had told him that if it wasn't for Jimmy and all the money he'd put into Tyson, which was actually quite meagre, he would throw the piece of shit's – those were his exact words – clothes out on the lawn and tell him to get the hell out because he's such a piece of shit. But he's tolerating things and allowing things to transpire under his domain that he'd never usually allow, ever, because of his friendship with Jacobs. You see, Cus couldn't say it was down to him, because then a man of that stature, a man of that cloth, wouldn't then be a man of that cloth. So for

Cus to keep his reputation, he had to say, 'I'm doing this because of Jim Jacobs. For my love and loyalty to Jacobs. Otherwise I would throw Tyson out.' And Cus said something racial, too, about Tyson that was pretty nasty and I don't even want to say.

KEVIN ROONEY: When Tyson allegedly made a pass at Teddy's wife's little sister [Rooney is mistaken: the girl at the centre of the dispute was Atlas's 11-year-old niece], Teddy pulled a gun on him. Tyson came down, saw Teddy, thought everything was going to be OK, and then Teddy put a gun to his head. And Tyson just looked at him. Teddy says, 'You think I'm kidding?' And that's when he shot the gun up in the air, by the tree. And Tyson walks right past him, into the gym, back down the stairs, out the front door, goes back to Cus's house and tells Cus, 'I'm going down to Brooklyn. I'm gonna get my boys to come up here and kill him.' And Cus took Tyson and shipped him back down to Bobby Stewart in Tryon to simmer down. So Cus really helped Teddy because Tyson was gonna go down to Bed-Stuy and get his boys. So there's a problem, and all of a sudden Teddy's putting a gun to his head. I mean, huh? I mean he only pinched someone's ass. So what? I'm sorry. I mean Tyson may have been lewd, and a little girl don't need that.

NADIA HUJTYN: Teddy did hold the gun to Mike's head. But Mike didn't do anything that bad. Don't get me wrong. Mike is terrible in that regard. But at that time Mike didn't do anything that bad. Mike wasn't that bad then. And Teddy was weird. You had to watch him all the time. Because you never knew what kind of mood he was going to be in, if he was going to take something out on you. And it's not true what Teddy said, about Cus just slopping around. That's not true at all. As a matter of fact, Cus said the only reason he stopped coming to the gym was because he wanted to give Teddy this outlet, because he knew Teddy was so self-destructive. I mean Teddy comes from a troubled background. His brother killed his grandmother. The reason he has that scar on his face is he was involved in an altercation with someone. He used to do that all the time. We all used to go out together and like I said you had to watch him all the time, because somebody would bump into him and right away it would be: 'Do I know you! Do I know you!' We've had this dysfunctional situation for all these years. And I don't want to… I don't want to be that way.

March 6, 1985
  W TKO R1 vs Hector Mercedes, Albany, NY
  Professional debut

April 10, 1985
  W TKO R1 vs Trent Singleton, Albany, NY

May 23, 1985
  W KO R4 vs Don Halpin, Albany, NY

June 20, 1985
  W TKO R1 vs Ricardo Spain, Atlantic City, NJ

July 11, 1985
  W TKO R2 vs John Alderson, Atlantic City, NJ

July 19, 1985
  W KO R3 vs Larry Sims, Poughkeepsie, NY

August 15, 1985
  W KO R1 vs Lorenzo Canady, Atlantic City, NJ

September 5, 1985
  W KO R1 vs Michael Johnson, Atlantic City, NJ

October 9, 1985
  W TKO R1 vs Donnie Long, Atlantic City, NJ

October 25, 1985
  W KO R1 vs Robert Colay, Atlantic City, NJ

November 1, 1985
  W TKO R1 vs Sterling Benjamin, Latham, NY

Mike was back at the house, back in his old room with the sheet and the old fight films. Except he didn't watch them so much any more. He was living his own film. Teddy was long gone. Kevin was training him now. Kevin was easier to be with than Teddy. But it didn't make much difference. It was all the D'Amato style. Cus was the main teacher, the inventor, and all the others were just ciphers. Jim and Bill had turned him pro and he was 11 and 0 after less than one year! Unbelievable! At nineteen years old! And he was getting attention in the press.

Bill was good at that, he had to admit. Jimmy was always good, of course, but Bill was sort of like the engine room. He was a cold fish but he was like the strategist. And now he was closing in on a title shot. He knew their plan. Youngest ever heavyweight champ. Younger even than Patterson was! The funny thing was that almost the hardest of them was the guy he fought on his debut, Mercedes, even though he knocked him out in a round. Boy, that guy came to fight. And they're supposed to give you a tomato can on your debut! The thing about the D'Amato style is that it gives you this confidence that you can handle anybody, that even on a bad night you'll have more than enough compared to the other guy, because of the style. He just won't know enough to beat you, however talented he might be.

Mike knew there were the three of them in Cus mythology – Patterson, Torres and him. But he added something extra that they hadn't had – intimidation. He could do that to people, and Patterson and Torres couldn't; that wasn't their thing, or maybe they weren't interested in it, but he was. And there was this one guy he fought – he'd been a good amateur – and this kid really was trying to make out that he thought he could win, but he was intimidated, too, Mike could tell, and so he just waited. He knew he could knock this kid out whenever the opportunity arose. So he bobbed and weaved and let the kid let go with all the punches born of this misguided false confidence, and soon enough the kid made a mistake, as he knew he would because he didn't have the tutoring of the style, and, bang, boom, a left hook. All over. Spectacular!

The other good thing was that he'd solved the problem that Cus had with him going back to Brooklyn from time to time. Well, why should he give it up? He knew a lot of people down there. He wasn't a slave. He was now a grown man. But Cus used to worry so much. OK, maybe sometimes when he went to Brooklyn he was a day or even two later than he'd said he would be. But then when he got back there was Cus, waiting up for him. And it made him feel bad. Now all that was solved, though, because of Steve. Steve did all his publicity. And Steve had an apartment right in the middle of Manhattan. Steve was very white but he was OK; there was no side to him. So he could go to Steve's apartment, then go to Brooklyn, then come back to Steve's, and Cus didn't worry because he knew he was at Steve's. Perfect.

But that was a minor thing, relatively. The main thing was that he saw these supposed heavyweight champions, like Holmes and Spinks, who were having this mini-series – and Holmes was just old and Spinks good, with a difficult, thought-out style, but still basically only a light heavy – and Berbick and the young guys they were writing about at the same time as him, like Biggs and Tucker. And do you know what? Not one of them worried him or gave him sleepless nights for one single second. He may only be 11 and 0, but he knew he could take every one of them out, even right now.

JOHNNY BOS: I just called whoever had the fighters. Mercedes was pretty game, actually, on his debut. I think they were all pretty game until they started getting scared. Mike Jameson had no fear of him. Afterwards he became one of Tyson's sparring partners. He was a big, durable guy. I got him Trent Singleton, John Alderson. Singleton had been a good amateur. Mark Young, I know I got. Conroy Nelson, I might have. David Jaco, I know I did. He had a knockout win over Razor Ruddock. A lot of these fights I was involved with but I didn't necessarily make the match. Jesse Ferguson, they made the match themselves but they asked me about him. Zouski, I got him. Mitch Green, I know I didn't get. They only gave him $35,000 and he was going fucking crazy at the weigh-in. You knew it was gonna be big, just because of the publicity they were sending out. Every time he fought they were sending out a cassette to every TV station in the United States. And another opponent, Reggie Gross, he wasn't scared and he isn't scared now. He's doing about ten fucking life sentences. [In 1989 Gross was convicted of three murders and given two life sentences.]

NADIA HUJTYN: The thing about the style is you don't have to think. The stimulus presents itself and you respond appropriately without conscious intervention. You just do it. It's absolutely perfect. The style is unbeatable if you execute it correctly. It wasn't just Mike that was unbeatable. It was his gift, his natural ability, with the style, that made it unbeatable and him unbeatable. He's the only one that beats him.

KEVIN ROONEY: José Torres – same style, but better than Floyd's. No question Tyson was the best of the three. I believe that Cus had continually improved the peek-a-boo style. That was all he did – reproduce this style. Then Tyson turned up. I turned up before, but I used to do all the same things. The principal job as Tyson's trainer was to remember what Cus taught me. And, yeah, Cus was always looking to improve the style. What we call 'the move' – stepping to the side and then throw the punch. Put ten-ounce gloves on him and start swinging. You know, Floyd just caught Cus's eye when he walked in the gym in New York one day. It was almost mythical.

Cus told me a lot of stuff... He was a very special person. He was very, very particular. When I was sparring down in New York, he showed me a picture, back from the '40s, which was when the Mob had a grip on it. He had a plan. His plan was to disorganise the Mob, the IBC [International Boxing Council] and Jim Norris. And it worked. Camille told me one time that Cus knew all the Mob guys. They grew up together.

Cus said he just ignored them – his childhood friends who grew up to be mobsters. She said he just ignored them. But Cus was very clever. He would make these mobsters, these Norris people, do what he was willing them to do in his mind. He never married Camille because when he was fighting the Mob they always used to threaten to kill your wife.

Cus wasn't paranoid. People say that about him, but he wasn't. They say he was a nut, but he wasn't. He was one smart guy. If he was so crazy, how did he make Patterson the heavyweight champion when he weighed 185lb? Then he comes along with Tyson, though he wasn't here to see it... If Cus had been there to see it, Don King never would have got him and he would never have left Bill after Jimmy died.

But Cus told me that his greatest achievement was with Floyd. Floyd was locked up in juvenile detention at a young age and then he came to the gym and Cus started training him. He came to Cus's gym, he was shy, he asked Cus to help him, 'cause there was a bully in the neighbourhood who was beating him up. So he wanted to learn how to box. He eventually beat the guy up, but more importantly he got up into that ring. But Cus never liked to talk about Floyd and Liston and all that, because Floyd went away from him by then. And when boxers go away from Cus, they go down. I got along with Jimmy, too. It was cool. He was my manager too and he made me a little money. For my last fight, Bill came down and Cus told him, 'Don't cut the money. Give him the money only when he's leaving.' 'Cause I was gambling then. 'Give him the money – all of it – when he's leaving.' That's how Cus was.

STEVE LOTT: When Mike was there at the house, they didn't have many fighters there. Once in a while they'd have sparring partners. Living with Cus was like living with a combination of a rocket scientist and a philosopher – the sense of brain power, for boxing. Anything else, he was completely disinterested in. Like, 'Can you help me hook up the stereo system?' No. But boxing, that was his forte. And the interesting thing that he did with boxing was he started to redesign it. And that is what is bad about boxing today, that the fighters are so brave, so courageous, but the stuff they're being taught is so elementary, so basic. There's no technique, because the teachers don't know.

Cus loved fighters' science. He picked up which punches land and which don't, and he devised the head motion. There was no urgency at the house. With Cus, the last thing he would've wanted was to have anything urgent. He wanted to build their confidence. He knew that the fighters were motivated by their emotions, whether it was in the home, driving a car, going to the grocery store. That confidence would carry over into the ring. And even if it didn't carry over a hundred per cent, it was a huge bonus.

In the beginning I know there were wars between Mike and Cus, and Mike wouldn't believe anything Cus would say and thought he was wacko, but I never talked to him about the early days. I was more concerned with what he was thinking then. Nobody on the planet knows more about boxing than Mike does. He's got a photographic memory. Fear as an emotion. It all became model stuff. Brilliant stuff. And he was interested because he loved Cus. And the fighters he looked at were the old-timers. When he turned pro, after the first fights in Albany, he would come down to the city for a day or two to have a break. I think the first time he might have stayed at a hotel but I said, 'Mike, what the hell, come and stay at my place.' Then, after that, after every fight he'd come. Fortieth St and Second Avenue. The same building as Jim Jacobs. It'd be a Friday, Saturday night, and I'd hear the bang, bang on the door and think, 'Shit, it's Mike.' Sometimes I might be entertaining some girl. But I'd let him in and we'd all spend the weekend together. We were very close friends. He was lovable and he was not a stupid guy. He was an all-out fighter, but no one in their wildest dreams thought he would become 'Mike Tyson'.

I'd come out of my bedroom in the morning and there on the couch would be my buddy Mike Tyson, who was sleeping. He was a good kid. Sometimes the previous night at about eight o'clock we'd order up a Chinese dinner or something. Then he would be gone. Sometimes when he came back in at three or four he'd walk over to the bed and shake me and say, 'Steve, warm that shit up. The Chinese food that we had left over in the refrigerator.' And I'd say, 'Nah, you do it.' And he'd say, 'Nah, you know how to cook that shit up, Steve.' It was like having a son. So you see Teddy was wrong. With drugs or with an alcoholic you need a certain amount of time. Teddy's version is: No, today. And when Mike comes to New York in '85 after the four years with Cus D'Amato, does he start hitting the street and beating up kids and stealing pocketbooks and cursing at people and being a bum? No, so Teddy was wrong.

November 4, 1985. Cus D'Amato dies, officially of pneumonia. It is, however, a death shrouded in secrecy to all but the inner circle. Tyson is said to be distraught, but goes back into action almost immediately, dedicating victories to D'Amato's memory.

JOSÉ TORRES: 'Moving the head' means moving the body, to the side. The metaphor for that was a train track. You don't want to get hit by a train. You move to one side or you move to the other side. If you move backwards, the train is gonna kill you. The strategy was to discourage the opponent from throwing punches. If the punch comes straight, you move to the side. If it's a hook, you bend down. You cannot move back. Pulling back is an invitation to get knocked out. But Tyson was a little messed up emotionally. No control emotionally. I had more control than Tyson, and so did Patterson. The thing that Cus did was teach him when to throw punches, and where to connect. To hit the guy when he's not looking, and hit him in the right spot.

Patterson is not OK now. He has Alzheimer's, very bad. Last legs. Four years ago you couldn't talk to him. He and Cus used to be close but Cus didn't want the Liston fights. Cus wouldn't let any of his fighters fight when he thought they could lose. That's why he was a good manager. The same way Liston beat Patterson, Ali beat Liston. No contest.

I like Teddy Atlas as a teacher more than I like Kevin Rooney, but I like Kevin Rooney as a person more than I like Atlas. Atlas is intelligent, smart, and he understood Cus better than Kevin did. Cus was very objective. If he liked you, and disliked me, but I was better than you, he would pick me. But Kevin was very loyal to Tyson. So Tyson's problem was emotional and Cus was expert at that. And Atlas said Cus just watched TV? That's funny. It happens so much in boxing that kids are uneducated but very smart. Tyson was a classic. I knew very early on that Cus would not take risks with him. He would make sure. We never found out if Camille and Cus had a relationship. Common sense says they did but Cus was so weird. Tyson used to call her 'Camillee'. But Tyson never got over Cus's death, because Cus was a father to him.

November 13, 1985
  W KO R1 vs Eddie Richardson, Houston, TX

November 22, 1985
  W TKO R2 vs Conroy Nelson, Latham, NY

December 6, 1985
  W TKO R1 vs Sammy Scaff, New York, NY

December 27, 1985
  W TKO R1 vs Mark Young, Latham, NY

January 11, 1986
  W TKO R1 vs David Jaco, Albany, NY

January 24, 1986
  W TKO R5 vs Mike Jameson, Atlantic City, NJ

February 16, 1986
  W TKO R6 vs Jesse Ferguson, Troy, NY

March 10, 1986
  W KO R3 vs Steve Zouski, Uniondale, NY

May 3, 1986
  W Decision vs James Tillis, Glens Falls, NY

May 20, 1986
  W Decision vs Mitch Green, New York, NY

June 13, 1986
  W TKO R1 vs Reggie Gross, New York, NY

June 28, 1986
  W KO R1 vs William Hosea, Troy, NY

July 11, 1986
  W KO R2 vs Lorenzo Boyd, Swan Lake, NY

July 26, 1986
  W KO R1 vs Marvis Frazier, Glens Falls, NY

August 17, 1986
  W TKO R10 vs Jose Ribalta, Atlantic City, NJ

September 6,1986
  W TKO R2 vs Alfonso Ratliff, Las Vegas, NV

DON MAJESKI: What I found about all of them up there was that they had this snobbery, this aloofness, that they're a group and that they're removed from everybody else. Yeah, before Robin Givens came along for Tyson it was like a monastery up there.

So, it was true. Cus was dead. Everyone had kept whatever illness it was away from him. It was all kept secret. And he'd had a fight a couple of days later. He went ahead with it, for Cus, And then another fight after that, and then another, and another. But it was just dawning on him, this huge vacuum that was at the house. Although Jimmy was trying to step into the breach, it wasn't really the same. And Jimmy and Bill weren't exactly matching him easily, despite what the press said. Mark Young could be dangerous but he'd dealt with him, comfortably. Jesse Ferguson was definitely dangerous, and then afterwards he'd said that thing about driving his nose into his brain that Jim and Bill were still pissed off about. And then they'd put him in back to back with Mitch Green and 'Quick' Tillis. Green had a severe attitude problem but, he had to admit, he hadn't been able to intimidate him beforehand. And Tillis was a good, clever boxer, just short of world championship material, but only just, and he'd dealt with him. Despite what the press had written, he was proud that he'd gone the distance with both of them and still won easily. It was like an old-time fighter would have done it. That's what he was thinking of. He probably didn't finish them for that reason. Like Joe Gans, going forty rounds at the start of the century. Now he'd had a taste of that.

He wished Cus had been there. He would have appreciated it. He would have known exactly what he was doing and why. It was like a horse at Belmont when they lull you with a few below-par performances. But Cus had told him all about that. And then you go out and win the big one, when they're gonna underestimate you slightly. Not that they would underestimate him, despite the press. He knew he was all the rage. And it was going to happen. Jimmy told him it would be Berbick, for the world title. And Berbick couldn't hit him on his best day. The women and the wine were more a problem than the fighters. Just like Cus said.

But this thing was more complicated, and Cus's death had brought it home. When you start off trying conning people to an extent, or maybe all it is, is that it's in the back of your mind, and then you spend years with them and attachments are formed. The person he felt most sorry for was Camille. She really cared for Cus, and she was the only one he felt really cared for him outside of boxing. All the other ones were just concerned with boxing, even Cus. But he would still take care of Berbick, for Cus.

After twenty-seven consecutive victories, Tyson signs to fight Trevor Berbick, a tough Jamaican, for the WBC heavyweight title in Las Vegas on November 22, 1986. If Tyson wins, he will become the youngest heavyweight champion in history, succeeding Floyd Patterson.

Part Two

THE CORONATION

STEVE LOTT: A couple of days before the Berbick fight I felt he might be nervous or whatever so I thought, 'Let me try this.' So we're driving back from getting a videotape and I said, 'Mike, I wanted to ask you a question. What do you think Cus would think about this guy?' That would make him third person and I knew he'd give a very accurate answer. And Mike said, 'He'd probably think he was a tomato can.'

November 22, 1986
  W TKO R2 vs Trevor Berbick, Las Vegas, NV
  Wins WBC heavyweight title

March 7, 1987
  W Decision vs James Smith, Las Vegas, NV
  Wins WBA heavyweight title

May 30, 1987
 W TKO R6 vs Pinklon Thomas, Las Vegas, NV
 Retains WBC and WBA titles

August 1, 1987
 W Decision vs Tony Tucker, Las Vegas, NV
 Wins IBF title and unifies heavyweight division

October 16, 1987
 W TKO R7 vs Tyrell Biggs, Atlantic City, NJ
 Retains all titles

January 22, 1988
 W TKO R4 vs Larry Holmes, Atlantic City, NJ
 Retains all titles

March 21, 1988
 W TKO R2 vs Tony Tubbs, Tokyo, Japan
 Retains all titles

February 1988. Tyson signs a series of contract assign-ments. Unbeknown to him, Jim Jacobs has been in and out of hospital with a mysterious illness. After the discussion regarding the contract assignments, in which Tyson shows no interest, he signs an agreement that in the event of either Jim Jacobs' or Bill Cayton's death, their joint managerial percentage will go to their wives. José Torres supervises and handles the contracts in his capacity as New York Athletic Commissioner. These contracts will later be used by Don King to persuade Tyson that he was being ripped off.

KEVIN ROONEY: Anyway, on the way back from the Tubbs fight, on the plane, I see Robin [Givens] has got a tight belly. And she's supposed to be four, five months pregnant. Now, my ex-wife, when she got pregnant, you see it almost right away. I was trying to get a message to Mike, 'cause Mike was there. So I say, 'Robin, you look great! Your stomach looks great!' And she says, 'Whaddya mean?' She was a bitch: 'I'm better than you. Who are you?' Like that. Ruth [Roper, Givens' mother] was a little warmer but she was still playing the game. They were both chasing Mike's money.

STEVE LOTT: Robin Givens was that moment. She sprang that wedge. Round about October of '87 he told me he was seeing her. In January of '88 she says, 'I'm pregnant to Mike.' I don't even know this. I went with him to Chicago to the NBA All-Star game, and we're about to leave for Tokyo in a week or two for the Tubbs fight. And he said, what would I think if he married Robin? I said, 'Great. Terrific.' Because at that stage she seemed kind and caring. Whatever she did, there was no baby. If she had married Mike and stayed warm and friendly and kind, I would have said fantastic. But the day they got married, Robin went to the offices of Merrill Lynch while Mike and I were in Tokyo. She was with her mother demanding the money.

José Torres came over about two weeks after we were there and the first thing he said was: 'Steve, we got trouble.' I said, 'What? Everything's great. Mike is training well.' [But] I knew something was amiss. And one time in Tokyo, maybe a week before the Tubbs fight, Robin was there for a couple of weeks but then she went back, and Mike comes into my room – he's just got off the phone to her or something – and he's sitting on the bed, and he said, 'I don't feel so good.' I said, 'What's up?' He says, 'It's Robin.' I knew she was driving him crazy because José Torres had told me. He's defending the title in three days and I've got to decide what to do, whatever he says. He says, 'I should never have got married.' I said, 'Mike, I guarantee you everything will be fine.' He said, 'You really mean that?' And I said, 'Mike, I promise you.' And he said, 'OK.'

JOSÉ TORRES: I was the best man at the wedding. I was one of the guys who was enthusing him to marry this girl. I thought she would straighten him out. But then I found out he was overwhelming her. He would push her around and slap her. So I call him up and I said, 'If I'm sitting next to you and Robin and I see you abusing her, I will hit you with a baseball bat. And if I kill you, I kill you, and I'm not kidding. You hitting that girl is so embarrassing for me. You're the heavyweight champion. Are you crazy?' But he was very co-operative with the book [Torres' 1989 publication *Fire and Fear: The Inside Story of Mike Tyson*], and I liked everyone in Tyson's group. The only one I didn't like was Tyson's wife's mother, Ruth Roper. She was very active, and she loved the attention.

We went to City Hall and I signed for him. I thought Tyson really loved Robin. It was one of his first experiences. Tyson's first girlfriend was a friend of my brother's daughter. But then in the ring he started to lose control also. That was awful, very bad. That was the thing missing. Without that fault he would have been the perfect champion of the world. And I didn't see Robin as a gold-digger. I thought she meant well for Mike Tyson.

NADIA HUJTYN: Everybody behaved in a certain way for Cus. I don't think Jimmy was the person that everybody thinks he is. I don't think he was the good, idealistic guy. I don't get that. Cayton had the money, for sure. Jimmy acted in a certain way because he thought he should, and I do think he cared more than Bill Cayton, because Cayton didn't care at all. Bill Cayton treated you like a possession, not like a person. But they didn't rip Mike off. They did show him the books, they tried to explain to him what they were doing, but Mike didn't want to know. He said, 'That's your job, not my job. I'll do my job and you do yours. I don't need to know about it.'

June 27, 1988
W KO R1 vs Michael Spinks, Atlantic City, NJ
Retains all titles

The Spinks fight was a piece of cake. And it was so huge! Every radio station was giving bulletins about it throughout the day. And the writers, at least a lot of them, were tipping Spinks! Spinks had no chance, and he knew it. Beating old man Holmes was no achievement compared to facing Mike. Spinks knew his style would rip him apart. And Spinks was really, really intimidated. And then he turned up with this ridiculous tuxedo at the press conference, as if he was a superior type or something. Mike did a very good job with the intimidation there. He was quite surprised by that, though. With Spinks being so experienced, even if it was mostly at light heavy, you wouldn't think he'd lose the plot like that. But, man, he did. Ninety-six seconds of the first round. He did catch him with this real shot to the body in the opening seconds, it was true. But then Spinks threw this big outrageous right hand – the Spinks Jinx, that's what he called it, just like Rocky Marciano called his right hand the Suzie Q. But it left him so open that he must have been looking to be knocked out, or at least looking to look like he was knocked out. In fact, that was what he thought Spinks was doing. Making it look worse than it was, just to get out of there. Maybe Spinks had too much money. Maybe he'd become a businessman more than a fighter.

TEDDY ATLAS: The Spinks fight did surprise me. Spinks was waiting for the bogeyman. He could have won that fight.

KEVIN ROONEY: Yeah, Spinks was scared. Cus

always used to talk about that. He said, 'Fear is your friend if you can control it.' Cus was so smart. I brought my daughter Amber up to visit him at the hospital. Then I brought Camille and his brother Tony, but Cus was out of it. It wasn't pretty, it wasn't ugly, it was just one of those things.

Following the brutal knock out of Berbick in two rounds, Tyson has grown to become the most sensational property boxing has seen for years. Jim Jacobs dies in somewhat mysterious circumstances, leaving a widow, Lorraine. Aware of Tyson's lack of fondness for Jacobs' business partner Bill Cayton, Don King is now hovering. At Jacobs' funeral, King, although uninvited, somehow inveigles himself to become one of the pall-bearers. In a shock move, Tyson then sacks Cayton, Rooney and Lott. Lawsuits follow. It is King who now holds the reins of Tyson's career.

February 25, 1989
  W TKO R5 vs Frank Bruno, Las Vegas, NV
  Retains all titles

July 21, 1989
  W TKO R1 vs Carl Williams, Atlantic City, NJ
  Retains all titles

And then they tossed him in with Bruno, and Bruno couldn't really fight, and so he hadn't trained maybe as much as he should have. But even if Bruno couldn't really fight, Jesus, he was strong. He was built like an Adonis. And he caught him in the first, a left hook. He lost his marbles for a second there. But Bruno was too scared to follow up. Bruno knew he shouldn't have been in there fighting for the world title, at least not against him. And Bruno also really bought into the intimidation line, big-time. Bruno wasn't that tall but he still was... big, somehow. Bigger than him. And also he was dirty. And those rabbit punches to the back of the head, they're the ones that hurt you and throw you off. The referee docked him points but Bruno didn't care. He was kind of intimidated but also not intimidated. Fights are complex things, with all sorts of emotions running around, not necessarily to do with abilities. Bruno was the sort of person you underestimated. He was fighting on adrenalin and fear. That fight was never gonna go more than five rounds. And it didn't. The press just kind of said, 'Yeah, he got rocked, but ultimately it was easy.' But it wasn't. He was fucking glad to get Bruno out of there, 'cause his conditioning wasn't right.

And then they tossed him in with Williams, but that really was easy, 'cause he knew all about Williams, having sparred with him down in White Plains back in the day, when he was just a kid and Williams was supposed to be the big coming thing, 'cause he'd been world amateur champion or something. But that don't necessarily make you a top-class pro. And he'd been aimed by Cus at the pros from the start. Strategically, and with all Cus's wisdom. That was his great advantage. Williams couldn't possibly match it. And he'd handled Williams back then, easy, and he was just a kid. Plus Williams was now shot. His chin had gone, everyone knew that. He probably had too many amateur fights. That can make you shot real soon into your professional career.

Cus was good on those types of things. He kept him up in upstate New York for most of his amateur career, because he didn't want him down in the city going up against some mean motherfuckers, and getting himself shot too early. Only when it mattered did Cus put him in. So yeah, Williams, one round. He didn't even bother to intimidate Williams too much, 'cause he knew it would be so easy. But he got in shape, still, 'cause the Bruno fight had taught him that he had to, 'cause he was there to be shot at by all these guys. And there had been changes. You see, now that Cus died and Jimmy died there was really only Steve and Kevin and Bill, and it really wasn't the same. And also sometimes they really got on his nerves. Like Steve, it could be oppressive. They were so... white. Pious, almost. Things shouldn't be like that, but there was no getting away from it. Brooklyn and Catskill were two different worlds. And white and black were two different worlds, too. And, anyway, he was with Don now.

KEVIN ROONEY: Actually, that Williams sparring session was the moment when Cus had confidence in appointing me as a trainer. We went out to White Plains and Williams was the up-and-coming name back then. I went there with a guy called Don. He died. He was smart at things like computers. He became friendly with Cus and he was like part of the extended family. So we came home, Don dropped us off, and Cus asked me what happened. I said Mike was using his jab and body shots and moving his head real good and Williams couldn't hit him. And Cus checked with Don and Don said exactly the same thing and that's when Cus had the confidence in me.

TEDDY ATLAS: The truth is far from what you get from a lot of people who have agendas, and you could say I have mine. But Cus died under strange circumstances. He died of pneumonia. Jimmy died afterwards. They said it was leukaemia but nobody ever documented that it was leukaemia. They both died in the same hospital. Pneumonia nowadays usually accompanies the last stages of Aids. All I know is that their records were kept confidential and hidden. They took no visitors. The hospital staff was very closed and secretive. You would think a president was in the freaking place.

And I remember other things. Like Tom Patti, who was at the house, and who later on tried to make some money trying to be the trainer keeping the Cus thing alive – Cus hated him! Cus used to call him a liar, which he wasn't more than anyone else. 'You're a liar! You're a liar! You're just like your father!' Because his father had fought for him and they had a falling-out. When they had the 14th Street gym, the Gramercy gym. Cus hated him. But two friends, Nicky and this guy Al, they came to Cus and asked him to do them a favour and take Tommy. So he came up but Cus couldn't hide his disdain for him. 'You're a liar!' And the kid would come to me and say, 'Teddy, I can't take this no more.' And when I left and was training fighters in New York, Tom came to me, came down and said, 'I hate Cus. I can't live there anyway.'

KEVIN ROONEY: You see, when Tyson enters the picture, Teddy gets jealous, I guess. Jealous of the attention that Mike was getting, because Cus put up a big banner in Main Street in Catskill, in '82, '83, when Tyson won the second amateur championship.

NADIA HUJTYN: I definitely thought that about Jimmy, that he was homosexual. I thought the wife, Lorraine, was just a front, and that actually he died of Aids. I never thought that about Cus, though. But as for Jimmy kissing Mike on the lips after fights, I don't think that's to do with that. Mike wanted that. He's a baby. He never grew up. He's a child. He's still a child. He wanted all the love and affection.

JOSÉ TORRES: He was very co-operative with that book at first. I made more money from that book than I made from any single fight I had.

In the book by José Torres, *Fire and Fear*, Tyson apparently confesses during a conversation with Torres

to wanting to hurt women during sex. In turn, Torres suggests to Tyson that he might be homosexual. Tyson strongly rejects this.

NADIA HUJTYN: I love José, but he doesn't understand, either. No one understands. You see, Mike wanted a role model, and you were the role model and he expected you to behave in a certain way, and José didn't behave in the right way. You see, José had his lovely wife Ramona – delightful, lovely person – but he also had this girlfriend. And Mike didn't like that. He used to get angry with José, and a lot of things in that book are a reflection of that anger. 'You're supposed to do things the right way because that's what I want.' And he was angry because people didn't.

Life's funny that way. He's not supposed to do the thing but you are. A lot of that stuff is one-upmanship with him and José. 'I did this.' 'Well, I did this also.' It all involved girls. José brought his mistress to the gym many times. That's how I know. He used to bring her to the fights and she would sit in a different place. I'm sure Ramona knew but she didn't deserve that, because she's a lovely person.

JOHNNY BOS: Torres' book, I thought was basically himself grandstanding about himself a lot.

DON MAJESKI: Yeah, so before Givens comes along it was like a monastery. And then all of a sudden the first woman comes in and Tyson falls apart. It's the virgin and the whore syndrome. She's a whore and a virgin at the same time. You're looking at her as some kind of angelic figure and at the same time you want to have sex with her. So you're trapped in this thing. You revere them and yet you want them, and that's what happened with Tyson. And boxing-wise he climaxed with Spinks. It was like Joe Frazier. After Frazier beat Ali, that was it. There was nothing left. Physically, emotionally, psychologically, he reached the point where he couldn't go any further. Frazier went through a couple of desultory fights against Terry Daniels and Ron Stander, then he got knocked out by Foreman. He was never the same. With Tyson, he beat Spinks and he could never be better.

The fame gets overwhelming. It's insanity. You talk about Hemingway, Fitzgerald, or like Marlon Brando – they reach a point where that iconic fame gets to them. Elvis Presley. It makes you crazy. The artistry has been compromised by the money. There's nothing left. You lose it. If Tyson retires after Spinks, then he's the greatest heavyweight champion ever. But Don King is brilliant in his field. Tyson was a vulnerable person looking for some kind of father figure. He'd had D'Amato. Tyson had corned everybody – Jacobs and Cayton, D'Amato and people in prison. But when he got to King he met his match, because nobody plays Don King except maybe the devil, and King played Tyson. King knew how to handle him and he trumped him at his own game.

NADIA HUJTYN: And Teddy became the narrator of the Tyson story because of his position – but there's something not right there. I don't know how he got there. I don't know if Steve and Bill helped him to shut him up. No, really. I don't know why because he doesn't really deserve to be there. He can't train people that well. He never could. He has his own psychological problems. I was there. I know what he did to me, for example. He used to take money from Cus, because he used to take the young boys – Cus always used to say 'boys', it was a term of endearment to him, 'my boys', they were mainly under the age of sixteen – and Teddy used to take them to New York and Spanish Harlem, which is a hundred and twenty miles and not a short hop if you drive. And he had a beat-up piece-of-junk car – so did I – and it was dangerous. It wasn't safe.

Teddy used to take money from Cus, unbeknown to me, for these trips. Now he didn't give it to me, but he took it, and we'd go down there, and I'd be lucky if he bought me gas, and let me tell you I didn't make much money then. I made barely enough to make ends meet. I couldn't really afford to make those trips. The money was supposed to facilitate us going there. So he took this money, and then one day Cus separated us. He sent me on an errand with some of the boys, and when I came back he had sent Teddy on the way already, and it was pouring rain, bitter cold, pitch-dark, and I was terrified to go there by myself. Spanish Harlem is a dangerous place. We used to go to this gym there, but we used to have to have this person across the street who ran a bar – we knew this person – to watch our car. That was twenty-six years ago. So that nobody would bother our car until it was time for us to leave. So he wanted me to go by myself and I said, 'Cus, I'm afraid. Why did you let Teddy leave? You knew I was coming back as quickly as I could.' And he said, 'Who comes first!' 'Who comes first?' I said, 'The fighters come first.' And he said, 'Well, what are you talking about? What's the problem?' I said, 'I'm afraid.' He said, 'Of what?' I said, 'What if something happened?' And he said, 'That's supposed to be taken care of.' And I didn't know what he meant.

I ended up leaving in tears. I went, and thankfully I got there, and I told Teddy and he says, 'Don't worry about it.' He says, 'I don't know what happened.' And I didn't get it. I asked Kevin and he didn't know. And I kept coming to the gym and Cus was awful to me. Cruel. Vicious. He wouldn't let me speak to anybody. He said, 'Now I know. Now I know.' It wasn't because I was a girl. The issue here is that he found out that Teddy was taking all this money from him, and apparently it was a lot of money, and Teddy told Cus he was giving it to me, when he was keeping it for himself. The reason Cus found out was because Teddy was also using his father's credit card and his father was calling Cus about the amount of money on the credit card, and Cus said, 'But I'm giving him money.'

And that's how I found out. So actually it worked to my advantage in the end. Because Cus knew that I was serious and blameless, and he couldn't apologise enough. So that's what Teddy did to me. And Teddy used to borrow money from me on top of that. And he was my trainer when I gave him the money. And Cus said, 'Did he pay you back?' And I said, 'Yes.' And Cus said, 'Well, he must really like you because he don't pay anyone else back.' He was a hoodlum, basically. I mean I had a pistol, and he wanted it once. And he asked for it, to carry it unlicensed, which I could get arrested for, because he was worried that some people were going to come after him and he wanted it for protection.

And as for Robin Givens, she was such an obnoxious bitch. Flat out. She didn't like Mike, not one iota. Why should she sleep with him? She didn't like him. Obviously it wasn't worth the money. If it was really worth the money, she would have had a child. That's the general route to get the money. So it wasn't worth that much to her. But Mike was ga-ga over her. Before he was: 'No girls will ever like me.' So he was in awe of her. They were worse than Don King. They went to Camille and they said to Camille, 'You've left the house to Mike, haven't you? You really should, you know. He's like your son.' And she said, 'Oh no, this is my house. This house is going to my sister. When I go, my sister gets this house.' But they had the gall to approach her. They were horrible people. Really horrible. It was all about money.

STEVE LOTT: At that point Mike and I were starting to… He didn't want any information from me. In fact one day I called him at the house out in Orangeville and said, 'Mike, why d'you buy the house? It's $4 million and you're going to need that money one day.' He says, 'Steve, I'm married now. I don't need your advice.' I said, 'Mike, you've always demanded that I tell you right from wrong.' And he said, 'Steve, you've gotta make me look good. I'm married. No more now.'

He knew really that I was giving him the right information. Like back in '86 he did an early morning TV show in New York. We go up there and he's wearing this sweater with a necklace on, a gold thing, and they're trying to put the microphone on him and I say, 'Hey, hold up, give me the necklace, Mike.' He says, 'Why?' And I say, 'Because it's my job and the necklace gives the wrong picture.'

A year later he's shooting the Nintendo commercial. He does the shoot and says to me, 'How did that go?' I said, 'OK, but you can do better.' He says, 'You can't tell me this shit, man. You just gotta make me look good.' But he did it again and it was much better. So he knew.

The key to the Robin Givens situation is this. When I'm with a woman, I don't even want to talk to anybody else. I don't want to see anybody else. With Mike, he comes back to New York, and he was training for the Spinks fight, and there's this incident where he's driving, she sticks her hand in his pocket and pulls out condoms. Now, why would he need condoms if he's married? So Robin realises he's fooling around…

In late 1988, Tyson is involved in a series of violent incidents. He crashes his Rolls Royce in New York after Givens reaches into his pocket and finds condoms. He has a street fight with a crazed former opponent, Mitch 'Blood' Green. He crashes a car into a tree outside the Catskill mansion and is knocked unconscious – an event Robin Givens and Ruth Roper portray as a suicide attempt. Police are called after Tyson smashes up the house, believing Givens to have had a sexual dalliance with the property mogul Donald Trump. The marriage disintegrates.

And Robin and him were finished. First there was the thing in the car. Then when they went to Moscow he could have killed her most of the time, she was playing up so much. Not literally killed, obviously. And she or her mother was leaking out to the press that he was slapping her around. The suicide thing when he crashed the car into the weeping willow at the house – that was just baloney. He just skidded. And then there were all these rumours about Donald Trump fucking Robin on his yacht. And he would confront Trump about that. That white motherfucker. And what was Robin's problem anyway? Was his dick too big for her? Then finally they went on the Barbara Walters show and Robin and Ruth drugged him up before-hand, with lithium. They said he was a manic depressive. And on air she just basically assassinated his character. Totally annihilated it. But the truth was he'd never really trusted her, or her mother. Well, maybe at the very start. After that he'd wanted to believe he could trust them. So much. He'd wanted to believe they were his family, like they said. But he realised he'd been deluding himself. And it was so hard now, because he loved Robin... even after the Barbara Walters show he was still deluding himself.

It took a few calls from friends, like Rory, to give him the wake-up call that he'd been made to look like a complete sap. That was how far gone he must have been in this madness. And then he started throwing furniture around and Robin or Ruth called the police and it was bad, man. But they left him alone. They didn't arrest him or anything. He just told them it was his furniture and if he wanted to throw it around it was his prerogative. The only good thing was Don. Don was cool. He knew what Don was after, of course; it wasn't hard to figure out – he was the heavyweight champion of the world for Chrissakes! – but it was still... respite, from the madness. And underneath Don's schtick there was a real person. And Don seemed to care about him a little bit. Seemed, of course. But sometimes 'seemed' is what it takes to get you through. And he'd been out to Don's place in Ohio and it was... sumptuous. He could do with something like that, once he got himself together again. And Don, whatever else he was really thinking, knew where he had come from. Don was from the ghetto himself, after all. And it was also true, even after all those years in Catskill, that he was still a black man, and like Don said, only a nigger knows what a nigger has to go through. You could... chill with Don, in a way you couldn't with Steve or Bill. Certainly not Bill. Jesus, why did Bill have to be such a cold fish? That was part of the whole problem.

But it wasn't as if he didn't remember Cus or Jimmy. He thought of Cus all the time, and the numbers and the words he used to call out when you were sparring. He would still fight in the Cus D'Amato style, that was for sure. And if he had a kid that's what he'd call it, D'Amato, whether it was a boy or a girl. So maybe he should stick with Bill. But what with Robin and Don and Bill, and firing Kevin, it was all such a mess and his head was... fucked. And basically Robin and Ruth just wanted to be white.

KEVIN ROONEY: Cus and Jimmy were not lovers. That's total bullshit. Cus loved Camille. That was his woman. Jimmy married Lorraine. That was his woman. They never had any sexual contact in any way, shape or form. Cus died of a rare case of pneumonia and Jimmy died of leukaemia which he had had for years and years. The real story is that one of the doctors didn't diagnose it and if he'd diagnosed it Jimmy would have lived. And I mean Cus was a MAN. And Jimmy was a man. And their sexual preferences were: they liked girls. But, yeah, when Tyson fired me I was shocked. I had no inkling. I was at

Madison Square Garden. People say that Mike was stupid but Mike was not stupid. He was smart. And that's why what surprised me even more was he got into bed with King.

NADIA HUJTYN: What happened was Kevin went on TV trying to defend the situation because people were saying bad things about Mike. He tried to say something placating. He said, 'They're two people. If people would maybe leave them alone to work out their differences… There's too many people trying to interfere.' And Don twisted that and went to Mike and said, 'Did you hear what he said?' – and that was it. King was like an ambulance chaser. He was waiting for that. He'd been waiting for that for a long time. And Kevin was devastated because he never thought it would happen. But Cus knew it would happen, and I have that on tape too. Cus told Mike – and Mike repeats it – Cus said, 'I know what you're gonna do. When you become heavyweight champion of the world, you're gonna be the egomaniac champion of the world and you're gonna tell me, "To hell with you. I don't want you any more."' And he may have if Cus had been alive because Mike is easily swayed. If Cus had lived long enough for Mike to have become a stronger person, then maybe he wouldn't, but he may have because he's too easily misled. You can twist everything and lead him away, and I don't know if he'd have the strength to come back, especially not to Cus.

CRAIG (Tyson's sparring partner in Catskill): I liked the sport of boxing, and a friend told me, so I came over and asked Cus. I had to go through the trials of sitting over there in the gym watching, for anything up to a month, Monday to Saturday. Cus would say, 'Who are you? Why do you wanna box?' The right answer was: 'Because I wanna be champ of the world.' I'd just seen it on TV and done a lot of street-fighting. It was 1981. I was nineteen years old. Me and Tyson pretty much came at the same time. You had to do everything just the way they said. Me and Mike were always the last ones to spar. We didn't start until about 8.30pm. Every sparring session was a fight. Mike didn't know how to take it easy. He never knocked me down but he broke my nose. Some mornings I woke up with blood on my pillow. Mike said I shook him a couple of times.

I was 25-3 as an amateur and won three state Golden Gloves. Teddy Atlas was a good trainer. He enforced the rules. With Mike, that's why I moved my head. If I hadn't, he would have taken it off! If he'd stayed here at the gym he would probably still be undefeated now. The punching is not what made him great. It was because he moved his head. But Mike gets frustrated and loses his concentration. Sparring with him was all about moving your head and jabbing and giving him a lot of movement. On the ropes he would kill you.

Kevin had him in court. Me and Mike used to be real good friends but then he got hangers-on. Rory

Holloway and that crew. Mike just wanted friends who were yes-men. Kevin getting fired was a shock to everyone. That's a case right there. When you say something that's the truth, Mike doesn't want to hear it. If he continues boxing, he's got to come back to his roots. He's got to learn the style again. It's in him already. If he stays with the people he's with, he'll never be champion. Nadia should be his trainer.

When he brought Jay Bright in for the Buster Douglas fight, Jay was just there to say the words. Now he doesn't even have that. But Mike held my babies a few times. I'm a correctional sergeant at Greene correctional facility. Mike came to my graduation ceremony and to my wedding. And we played around with Camille's dogs – Prince and Duran. Then he started having nice cars. That's when the so-called friends started coming in. They started driving up in these new Corvettes. The only thing I got from sparring with him was complimentary tickets. I never asked him for anything. It was loyalty to Cus.

NADIA HUJTYN: Brian Kenny, who now works for ESPN2 with Teddy, he interviewed me after Mike left us and said, 'What's going to happen?' And I said, 'Mike is going to lose.' He just had the Spinks fight. And I said, 'He's going to lose.' And he says, 'Well, because I know you and respect you, I won't laugh, but everybody else is gonna laugh.' It was before the Bruno fight. And he said, 'Why do you say that?' And I said, 'Because Cus said it. And Mike knows

Cus said it and he knows what Cus said is true. Cus said, "A person who compromises his principles, who compromises what he believes in, cannot succeed." So therefore he has to lose.' And Mike knew it, just like he knew everything else Cus said was true.

Don't forget, Cus worked hard with him to make sure he had no doubt about being heavyweight champion of the world. Mike knew, beyond a shadow of a doubt, that he was going to be heavyweight champion. Think about it: you have no doubt. Erase all self-doubt. Cus worked very hard to ensure that there was no doubt. We all knew that he was going to be heavyweight champion of the world. Everybody in the gym knew. In fact, it wasn't as exciting as it might have been because we knew. It was a foregone conclusion if everybody did their part. And that's why he had to lose, too. And he did. It took just three fights.

STEVE LOTT: Then Mike had an about-turn. He broke up with Robin Givens over the Barbara Walters show, and then he came back to the office and apologised to Bill Cayton about having said those things with Don King. He said, 'I'm sorry,' and Bill said, 'Forget that. It's history, what's important now, Mike, is you. I'm going to bring in the world's greatest psychiatrist to examine you and I want you to come down here at noon tomorrow for the appointment.'

The guy came in, Mike came in, he examined Mike and said, 'This boy's sad but he's fine. Who pronounced him a manic depressive?' 'Cause Robin

Givens had this doctor give him lithium. Dr Henry McCurtis. The doctor who examined him for us was Dr Abraham Halpern. So Halpern calls McCurtis. 'Hello, I am here with Mr Mike Tyson and I hear you prescribed him lithium. You gave it to Robin to give to Mr Tyson? I don't understand. How could that be done like that? This boy is no manic depressive.'

So Dr Halpern pronounces him fine, and Bill said he was going to get him fights in Italy against Damiani, in Brazil against Rodriguez, while he got his life together after Robin – and that's where I made my big mistake. I wasn't smart enough to stick with him and say, 'Mike, life is gonna be great again.' Instead he said, 'See you guys later,' and walked out the door. And Don grabbed him the next day, and that was it.

Part Three

THE FALL

February 11, 1990
 L KO R10 vs James 'Buster' Douglas, Tokyo, Japan
 Tyson is defeated for first time and loses all titles

The tenth-round defeat by Buster Douglas, after a previous shaky display against the limited Frank Bruno, is catastrophic. It is made worse by Don King's initial attempt to have the result reversed, on the grounds that when Douglas was floored in the eighth round – one of the few good moments for Tyson – the count was long. During the fight, Tyson's corner work is shambolic. King brought in a new trainer, the rookie Aaron Snowell. Presumably at Tyson's request, the chief second is his former friend from the Catskill house, Jay Bright, not previously known for boxing expertise. When Tyson's eyes begin to swell from Douglas's incessant jabs there is not the appropriate equipment in the corner, and Snowell attempts to reduce the swellings by applying a condom filled with ice.

TEDDY ATLAS: And then along came a guy called Buster Douglas who didn't sign on the dotted line. For once it was: 'He's going to have to vanquish me.' You see, Tyson never really vanquished people. They vanquished themselves.

Shit, that was bad, man. He wasn't expecting Douglas to be like that at all. He could see that Douglas was in shape, more than he'd noticed before, but he hadn't thought it would make any difference. Although hadn't Mickey Duff, the English guy who advised on some fights, once said to Jimmy, 'Don't fight Douglas. If he's in shape, his style's all wrong for Mike'? But Douglas was supposed to lie down. He thought he would. He had this reputation for giving up. Like with Williams, he didn't even bother to intimidate him. Having said that, Douglas didn't really seem intimidatable, to be truthful, 'cause his mother had just died, and he was riding some wave of I-don't-give-a-fuck emotion. He was unlucky to have caught Douglas in that state.

But maybe he wasn't in the absolute best of shape. Things were different under Don. The corner was actually embarrassing. This guy Aaron Snowell, who was supposed to be his trainer, who he hardly knew! And Jay! Jay in his corner, for a world heavyweight title fight! How the hell do you come to that? His idea was just for Jay to say the Cus numbers, words. But Jay?? They didn't even have the endswell to bring down the cut over his left eye. They had – can you believe it? – some condom from someone in the corner that they filled with iced water to try and reduce the swelling. But it didn't work. Well, why the fuck would it? Boxing's been going on for over a hundred years and so far condoms haven't been used to control cuts.

And he felt flat-footed. Really strange. He couldn't get the style back. And Douglas is peppering him – jab, jab, jab, right hand – and he can't seem to get himself going, at all. So he's just got to wait for an opening, a mistake, and then in the eighth he got it – an uppercut, flush. And Douglas goes down, and Mike was looking round the referee, to see if he would get up. He didn't think he would, but he did. Jesus, this Douglas was maniacal that night. And he knew he was finished. Because he could see from his face that Douglas wasn't going to stop once he got up. And he couldn't take it any more, the peppering with the jabs and the right hands that were going straight into his wounded eye.

So in the tenth he's on the canvas, grasping for his gumshield. You can't say he wasn't game. And Don tried to say afterwards that there was some sort of illegal long count, when he'd put Douglas down in the eighth, going to commissions and the WBC et cetera... And that was embarrassing too. Douglas had won fair and square. And he'd lost. He'd lost. He'd lost...

NADIA HUJTYN: He left! It's very hard to maintain that style on your own. You need the people to say the words. To fix your foot by half an inch. To fix the line of the body. If you're sloppy about it, it doesn't work. If you don't time it correctly, it doesn't work. That takes careful attention to detail. Nobody else knows it. People try to approximate it but they don't understand the timing. They don't understand the purpose. The style is unbeatable if you execute it correctly. But Mike left!

JAY BRIGHT: Mike had changed a lot. He wasn't a high-school kid any more. And as you grow up and grow older you have different people around you, different situations. You don't think the way you do as an aspiring fighter or teenager when you're up there and on top of the world. So I think he changed in that degree. In certain aspects, but not all aspects. In certain aspects, he was still the congenial, nice guy that he always was. I've taken the heat for the Douglas fight for years. Basically the misconception that most people have is that I was the cut man. I wasn't. Unfortunately the cut man didn't have the endswell and didn't have what was necessary to control the cut or the swelling. But I just take the heat and that's it.

KEVIN ROONEY: Jay Bright was nothing. He had nothing to do about nothing. He lost both his parents and Cus and Camille took him in. He was never really Tyson's trainer [in fact he was, later on]. He was a second. He used to argue with Cus all the time about stupid stuff. They didn't talk for about a year. Jay was a slob. He didn't come into the picture until after Cus was dead and Tyson left me. Aaron Snowell came from Don King. He was another asshole.

STEVE LOTT: I should have said, that day at Bill's office, 'Mike, wait for me out there.' Then I should have gone to Bill and said, 'Bill, write me a cheque for $100,000 so I can take him down to Brazil for a couple of weeks.' I should have said, 'Bill, he's in bad shape. Let's take him down to Rio, let him get laid about sixty-six times a day, and after four weeks his mind will be off Robin.' Let me tell you – if the woman of my dreams left me and someone took me down to Rio, it would take my mind off it. Maybe it wouldn't be that great but it would still be better than being by yourself. And after four weeks it would have been: 'OK, let's go.' But instead of Rio it was Buster Douglas in Tokyo. Don got him when he was an emotional wreck, took him up to Cleveland, and then it's: 'Mike, let's take a look at those contracts.'

You see, you have an illness, you go to a doctor. But Don King is not your average doctor. He's the master doctor. Mike had been crushed by Robin. If it had happened six months earlier it would never have happened the way it did. It's very difficult for the public, even the boxing public, to understand that emotionally he was drained going in against Douglas. All that stuff was reverberating around his brain. And Douglas was the most relaxed opponent he had faced. By round two Mike was totally drained. It was the Robin Givens–Don King one-two, followed literally by the Buster Douglas one-two. And you know what I remember about it all? I remember before the Biggs fight, he was sleeping at the apartment, and I said to meet outside the Trump Plaza and I saw him walking up 42nd Street, the heavyweight champion of the world, in jeans and a T-shirt, serenely at peace, not a care in the world.

NADIA HUJTYN: Mike just wanted Jay there to say the words.

KEVIN ROONEY: If Mike had still been with me, he would have knocked Douglas out in a round or two.

STEVE LOTT: If Mike went to Don King and Kevin was still the trainer, he would still have lost to Buster Douglas. If he thinks he's hated or despised, he will not be able to fight. He's so sensitive to how people think about him, he will not produce in the ring.

June 16, 1990
  W KO R1 vs Henry Tillman, Las Vegas, NV

December 8, 1990
  W TKO R1 vs Alex Stewart, Atlantic City, NJ

March 18, 1991
  W TKO R7 vs Donovan Ruddock, Las Vegas, NV

June 28, 1991
  W Decision vs Donovan Ruddock, Las Vegas, NV

Don brought him back with two one-round knockouts, and people thought they were knockovers but they weren't on paper, actually. They both had severely winning records. Henry Tillman he got his revenge on from the amateurs but it didn't make him feel good because Henry and him went back a long way and he was a nice guy. But he was shot and intimidated so he just got Henry out of there as soon as possible to spare him unnecessary misery and dread. Then came Alex Stewart, this Jamaican who just wasn't good enough to cope with him. He was intimidated, plus he caught him early. And then Don got him back-to-back fights against Razor Ruddock, and that wasn't doing him any favours, 'cause Ruddock was another of those big, strong motherfuckers who were always bigger than him. And he'd started trash-talking more. Jail talk, basically. He'd told Ruddock that he'd kiss him on his big lips! That was funny. Well, if they thought he was an ape, he'd fucking act like one. And he knew why Don had had to get him Ruddock. Because Douglas had got high on the hog and got fat and laid down against Holyfield, who was moving up from cruiserweight. And Holyfield had the wrong connections. They were out to keep Don frozen out. And now the heavyweight division was out of Don's control for once.

Amazing, wasn't it?! He hooks up with Don King, the great promoter of the Rumble in the Jungle, and it's the first time in about twenty years that Don didn't have a lock on the whole golden cage. So now he was out of the picture. Typical. But he knew things would turn. They always did, and with Don's energy, they always would. And he was box office, man. Sometimes he could hardly believe it, but he was. Huge box office. But they would have to wait, and he'd have to keep himself together. And he would. And he'd dealt with Ruddock both times. It wasn't exactly easy, and Ruddock hadn't really been intimidated, but Ruddock was basically just a slightly higher-grade Bruno. He was heavy-handed but he was pretty slow and couldn't really box at his level. Yeah, but he was a stubborn motherfucker, the type of opponent who can take it out of you even if you beat them. But he'd done it, and come through.

Also he'd had a kid, a little boy, and he'd called him D'Amato just like he said he would, and although he wasn't seeing his mother any more, he'd always let him know he loved him, throughout his life, and give him money of course. He would do the right thing, or try to. But he was spending bad, man. It was almost like a dream. And the women... You go out with a limo and a driver and they just get delivered to you, the women. He didn't know what it was costing him. Maybe nothing. Maybe they just liked him. So many, it was actually ridiculous. And once he and Rory had had twenty-six hookers between them in one day. One after another. Well, he gave himself one hundred per cent to Robin and look what happened. He could do what he liked now. His only regret was that he'd told José Torres about the twenty-six hookers and José had printed it in his book. But Don had long since told him not to deal with José. It was all history... ancient history.

The main thing was to keep himself together, which he was doing, and also earn some money for his boy D'Amato from fights, to compensate for the spending. But Don was working on the Holyfield connections and he knew that was going to happen, for sure. He didn't really want to do it any more, to be honest, the magic of it had been... extinguished. But you had to take your adult responsibilities seriously, man. Well, you had. And Holyfield would be easy, real easy, because for once Holyfield would be a smaller opponent, much smaller – for once! – and it would be for a real pot of gold, and if he remembered even ten per cent of what Cus had taught him, Holyfield couldn't live with him for one second. But then just when Don had arranged Holyfield there was the rape thing in Indianapolis. This beauty pageant 'queen'. And as far as he could recall, it was all bullshit.

Despite a couple of easy knockouts, Tyson is frozen out of the heavyweight title scene. Buster Douglas, in abject shape, loses his titles by knockout to Evander Holyfield. Don King has no promotional options for Holyfield, either, and unprecedentedly is in the heavyweight wilderness himself. Tyson remains the biggest draw in boxing. But to get him the big TV fights, King has to match him with the contender everyone else is avoiding: the dangerous Donovan 'Razor' Ruddock. On

the way back from winning the second Ruddock fight, in early July 1991, Tyson stops off in Indianapolis to act as a judge for the Black Expo beauty pageant. With his current girlfriend unavailable, Tyson, who had been drinking all day, invites one of the beauty contestants, Desiree Washington, to his room at the Canterbury Hotel at 2am. The following day, Washington files a claim that Tyson has raped her. Tyson is tried, convicted and sentenced to six years in jail.

NADIA HUJTYN: I have a theory about the women. With boxing you get this adrenalin high, and there's only one other place to get it. So it's the same type of high. That's what he's looking for. And he's looking to feel better, but that only lasts so long, so you have to do it again, so you feel better again. Mike is all about how he feels. You can talk to him, you can think he's very sensible, that he understands what you say, and then he goes out the door and something happens and he gets upset, and he does whatever it takes to make him feel better and completely forgets what you were talking about.

DON MAJESKI: Tyson would make a pass at anything. And Rooney would make a pass at anything.

KEVIN ROONEY: Ruth Roper, Robin's mother – I tried to pick her up and Tyson got all pissed off about it. I denied it but I did try to pick her up. And Mike comes up to me and says, 'What were you hitting on my mother-in-law for?' So I said, 'I wasn't.' But I was. But she didn't want it.

COURT TESTIMONY OF DESIREE WASHINGTON:

Q: Did he ever strike you?

A: No, he just held me down.

Q: Did he ever threaten to strike you?

A: No.

Q: Was there any weapon involved?

A: No.

Q: Desiree, has what you've told me here been the truth?

A: Yes. I gave it because of the fact that he could be doing it to other girls. And it's hard for me to do this because of who he is, but when I think about it, he could be doing it to younger girls than me. And it upsets me because he is a black man who basically came from nothing and who rose up and... I am one who advocates black people helping each other and not pulling each other down. But he's doing this to me. He could be doing this to other girls... black girls or white girls, it doesn't matter. No one deserves this.

COURT TESTIMONY OF MIKE TYSON:

Q: Mr Tyson, at any time did you force Desiree Washington to engage in sexual intercourse with you?

A: No, I didn't. I didn't violate her in any way, sir.

Q: Did she at any time tell you to stop what you were doing?

A: Never, she never told me to stop, and she never said I was hurting her. She never said 'No', nothing.

Did he rape her? Well, shit, he certainly never meant to. He never thought he was, at any stage, even during it. It was all such a fucking haze. He'd been drinking beer all day. And then you just get Dale, the body-guard, to call the girls. But maybe she was different from the normal type of girl he was with. Even though she showed him pictures of herself in the swimsuit competition. But maybe that was it. And there was all this Christian shit going down, even though Don was getting him baptised. But still... And maybe really, like Dale said, she just got pissed off that he didn't walk her downstairs to the limo. Well, Christ, he offered her to stay the night. He could have done with her there, is the truth, just to have a warm body next to you. It's like the couch, man, although he would never admit that to anybody.

The crazy thing was that he had a woman already, in town. But Angie wanted to see her folks, and he didn't want to get involved in that shit. And when he was on bail Angie wouldn't want to see him no more, because she knew he'd slept with Desiree. And Angie was really, really hot. But then Desiree did the big grandstanding performance. In court, for fuck's sake. Rape. So it was all complete madness again, and now he was in jail. But you know the funny thing? It's not so bad. A couple of the warders are assholes but you expect that.

And he was safe. In jail, you're basically safe. Well, if you're some weak-ass puny white guy you might not be safe. But as the former – and future –

heavyweight champion of the world, you're safe. And you get the visitors. From all over the world. He had to fend them off, and pull out from the list who he would see. Some strange people. Some of them he saw. Well, the whole thing about jail is passing the time. But apart from the strangers it was mainly the boxing operators. Most of them didn't have a hope with him. He knew that Don was on a different level, but it was good getting the attention. You see, if you know jail, even from way back, when you were a kid, you... actually like it in a way.

The worst thing, obviously, is the time. Getting through it. And there's this Islamic guy, a preacher or something, and he's been talking to him and that's good. As well as passing the time, it's good. He's an OK guy, this preacher. And he's started wearing the skull-cap and everything. That's funny, in a way! Converted to Islam, man. That's fucking unbelievable. But what white middle-class people don't understand is that the black Muslims run the jails, or at least their own wings, and that's how you survive. It's easier to do it than not to. Not that he didn't have privileged status. Everyone knew who he was. Was anyone really going to mess with him?

And he was keeping abreast of the heavyweight situation. The only one coming up was this Lewis, another big motherfucker. Really big. With this kind of Eastern European style which could be difficult to deal with, but it was surmountable. Apparently that's how he was taught in the amateurs. And he'd won the

Olympics and everything. Beat Bowe. But everyone knew Bowe was shot already. Like he said, too many amateur fights and you get shot. So when he got out he'd take Holyfield first and then he'd take out Lewis.

DON MAJESKI: I lived through the '60s and the Muhammad Ali era, and we now have made him America's secular saint. Tyson is America's secular demon. They've both ended up on on different sides and neither one deserves the title that's been imposed on them by the intelligentsia. They like to make boxers bigger than they are. Look at today's world. There's no way the Muslims are pacifists. So why didn't Ali go to Vietnam? He wanted to alienate society. It wasn't enough just being black, so he did something radical. He didn't believe the war was wrong. He did it because Elijah Muhammad told him to do it. He was a complete pawn. If Elijah Muhammad told him to jump off the Empire State Building, he'd have done that as well. He had no intellectual beliefs of his own. He was just used by this organisation, which was basically a black racist organisation.

Tyson converting to Islam was more of a fuck-you to society. How religious a Muslim is Mike Tyson? He's got Mao Tse Tung tattooed on him, a communist, as bad a killer as Hitler. He's got Arthur Ashe tattooed on him. I don't think Tyson knows what he wants to do. He's in search of an identity, that's the problem. Now I think Ali is a far greater person than Tyson, but we've changed him into something he never wanted to be, never said he was. We just invented this image of this guy, like he's Mahatma Gandhi or something. He belonged to boxing. After three and a half years he was theirs, meaning he was politicised. He was no longer part of boxing. He went beyond that. They made him something he never was and never meant to be. And with Tyson, that's what they tried to create again. But then you have the Palookaville rape. Now whether or not he raped the girl, there's nothing political about that. They wanted to make him political. I think Tyson's probably apolitical. He became a Muslim but he might as well have become Jewish. There's no religious conviction with Mike Tyson.

FRANK MALONEY (manager of Lennox Lewis and Julius Francis): Then Tyson was in jail, and you had to feel sorry for him in a way. You had to think, was some of the stuff manoeuvred to get him in jail? I think certain people wanted Tyson locked up.

In a surprise move just days before his release from an Indiana jail, Tyson re-signs with Don King. However, he is also to be 'managed' by two friends, Rory Holloway and John Horne.

And Don he would keep more at arm's length. But for various reasons Don was very difficult to keep away. At least he would have his own independent management. Rory suggested it. Rory and this guy from Los

Angeles, John Horne. He was a kind of fly guy. He was a stand-up comedian but in all truthfulness he wasn't actually that funny the times when he'd seen his act. What he really was, was a fixer. So he could be useful to him and he could be relied upon. And also it would be fun. Three young guys taking on the boxing establishment, even Don maybe!

It really pissed him off when the writers said Don was just his 'new father figure'. As if he needed one. It was different from Cus. And it was true he'd once asked Camille if he could introduce her as his mother, which must have looked strange to other people sometimes, but who really gives a fuck what other people think? That was what he needed at the time, and Camille saw that and said, 'Yes.' But for the moment he probably needed Don, and also Don had some deal in the offing with this new Vegas casino, the MGM Grand, that was going to make him humungous sums. Humungous. So he walks out of jail and the scene is just crazy. Hundreds of journalists, TV crews, the works. And Don is there and Rory and John are there. But he insisted to them that they go to the mosque first, with this preacher guy, and Don looked kinda funny with his shoes off.

And then he went back to Ohio but now after a few months of being out he was spending more time in Vegas, too. And he was going to buy a house there, too, a big fuck-you house. And he'd get a tiger – yeah! – a pet tiger. But that wouldn't be for show. He would treat it with love, 'cause animals and humans have basically the same feelings, that's what people don't understand. So, yeah, John was doing his fixing, particularly with the girls. He just delivered them to him and Rory, and that was very cool. John wasn't so interested himself. Sometimes they just did them in the back of the limo. It wasn't like he was forgetting the old days with Cus. He never would. But Cus had gone and then Jimmy went and sometimes you just had to move on. And after four years in the slammer you were entitled to enjoy life. And the best thing about this MGM deal was that the opponents were going to be tomato cans, but for title-fight money – at least the first few before he fought for the titles – so you had to give it to Don, he really conned those MGM guys. And it was sweet, cruising the Strip in Vegas, going to the clubs with John and Rory – OK, the strip clubs mainly – but yeah, it was sweet. But he would always see Camille and make sure she was all right.

DON MAJESKI: Really, decadence set it. Horne and Holloway were cruds. Money didn't mean anything to Tyson so if he wants to give these guys half a million a year, so what? It was insanity. King, Tyson – it was all crazy.

TEDDY ATLAS: I ran into Tyson a couple of times later on. We had a couple of situations. The most hair-raising was when he was world champion and still not completely exposed, not only as a fighter but as a human being, and he still had some endorsement power and he was shooting a Japanese beer commercial at Gleason's gym in Brooklyn. I was training a fighter in Gleason's. They closed it down for that day but if you were one of the guys of good standing there you could go in and train your fighter and stay in a certain area. So I knew he was going to be there and the last thing I wanted to do was be in that gym. But you got to put your money where your mouth is. So I went to the gym to meet my fighter, without saying a word to him or anyone. But I'm not devoid of being aware of what's going on. I knew there was a chance we'd meet.

So there's all this camera stuff going on. We're supposed to be to the side. And I go into the back. I was one of the only guys who had that kind of locker. I had a thing going with a guy called Joey Fariello, God bless him, and Joey wanted to be partners with me. He hated Gleason's. Hated it. He said, 'There's such scum in there.' Now I'm not a genius but I do know the time of day and I kept a steel bar in my locker. There were different things and I always used my hands but, whatever... you never know when a bar might come in handy.

So I opened up my locker in the back room and I can almost feel the chill of that room as I'm thinking about that day. There wasn't many lights on. It was dark and I'm getting my stuff out of my locker and I got my bag down. There's nobody in the back and I know Tyson is in the building. It was just me. And anything can happen back there, to be quite honest with you. It was a little bit detached from the gym.

I had my back towards the door. Well, there's no door, it's just an opening. And I just had a feeling. The hair on the back of your neck, whatever you want to say... At the last second, as I'm about to turn, I take the bar. I stand it up and I put it right against the door of the locker where it was easy to grab but it was still out of sight. And just as I turned Tyson was there and he'd got as close to me as he could without me turning. I turned around probably just as he was going to take the last few steps. He was about five yards away from me. And I turn around and there's nobody else in the place and he's the heavyweight champion of the world now. And I stare at him. He stops and he stares at me. I have to assume he saw me walk in. But, maybe he was going to the bathroom. I don't know. We didn't have much chatter.

So we're staring at each other and immediately I realise I have to do something. Because if I leave it like this... I know physically what he's got. But without being corny I also know what I am and what I will or will not tolerate. And I will not tolerate living in a way that I can't deal with. I mean, everyone wants to live but you have to live under conditions and terms that are appropriate to a man. That was the only thing that mattered to me, despite any other fears that were creeping around. He was just staring at me with disdain and bad intentions. He was trying to make a decision about what he was going to do. I didn't just want to be a good gallant soldier. I wanted to win. At least I knew I wasn't going to lose in a way that I couldn't live with. I wasn't going to do that. But I wanted to win on another level, too. I knew that if I just stood there any more seconds that would give him the confidence, the smell that he needed.

So before that second ticked away I took like two steps towards him. I actually measured my steps because I wanted him to know that I was ready to go, but I shortened up my gait where I was actually only one step and one arm's length from the bar in the locker. And I looked right in his face and I said something without actually saying it. And what I was saying was, 'I ain't no different, and you ain't no different. You might be heavyweight champion of the world now, and you might be a bit bigger' – 'cause he was 230lb by then instead of 210 – 'but what meant something to me then, what meant the whole world to me then, still means the same to me. And where I will go, and not go, is still the same.'

It seemed like we were there for a few minutes but it was probably only about twenty seconds, but when I took those steps and I stared right into his pupils, and he stared into mine, my weight was on my back foot, because I didn't want to waste a second, and I was like a spring. I was like coiled, 'cause I was gonna do some damage to the best I could. And then all of a sudden he just put his head down and turned around and walked out. And that was the end of it.

And you know what? The whole rest of the day I trained my fighters. And the whole rest of the day and the next day, too, I was trying to remember… It was so strong what we went through… I was trying to remember whether I actually said the words, or I just thought them. I wasn't sure if I'd said them. For a whole day I was confused. And the words were: 'What the fuck you gonna do? That ain't gonna do shit for you, standing there. What the fuck you gonna do?' I never said it, but it felt like I said it. But I think he heard it.

STEVE LOTT: After Spinks, nothing. No contact. And it was brilliant of King to put those people around him when he came out of jail. Because the more Mike was around them, the more Mike would act like them and the less likely it was that Mike would turn round in his own mind and say, 'Enough is enough. I'm going back to José Torres or Kevin Rooney.' It was an emotional wall and King knew Mike was the type of a guy who would not have the deep inner strength to say, 'I made a mistake.' He knew Mike would rather die, and be laughed at and despised, than to say he made a mistake. It's that street ghetto mentality. If you and me are talking about a woman, and she's dating another guy, you don't say, 'I'm going to ask her why she left and then I'm going to try and get her back.' No, you say, 'That bitch, I'm not gonna be with that girl any more. You're right.'

Mike was on a pedestal again. White people are no good. Don is brilliant at it, and while the president has about sixty-six advisors to inform him about everything, Mike had no one but Don, who was telling him all this stuff. Mike was in the hole, and the more stuff he was saying, the more he got in the hole. Don is the master at it – Ali, Witherspoon, Chavez, Gomez, ABC Sports. He's a brilliant conman.

KEVIN ROONEY: King had Rory Holloway and John Horne for his Tyson plan. Holloway is from Albany but I never see him around. Those are the guys King had with him when Tyson got out of the can. And then it was totally downhill.

STEVE LOTT: When Mike was with us, his mind was right there. With Don he was worried about the press. He knows he screwed over Bill. In the ring maybe you can't see this at first. But when I looked at Mike I knew he was disturbed emotionally. The opponent was the last thing Mike was thinking about. It was all outside-the-ring stuff.

KEVIN ROONEY: Tyson in some respects became an asshole, that's what happened. So for me it was like: 'Fuck you, if you want to be an asshole, be an asshole.' It wasn't about fucking money, it was about principle. Tyson had his head up his ass. I think basically he's a good kid. But he went down the aisle with Don King and King is a prick. King is not lazy and I'll take my hat off to that, but he doesn't do it the right way. He's a fuckin' bookie from Cleveland.

STEVE LOTT: I went out to visit him in jail three times, when he was in Indiana. I'd been hoping he'd say, 'I made a mistake.' But it was easier to say that white people are no good and black people have always been taken advantage of. But I was hoping and praying that he would do that and reach out with his heart and say, 'Steve...' And he did say it once, in a way, when he was in Indiana. What happened was I kept writing letters without getting a response. And some friend of mine said, 'Get a visitor's permit from the warden and they'll clear it.' So I go out there – big room, a table, the door opens up on the other side and Mike comes out. Minimum security, no leg irons. I don't think anyone wrote him more letters than I did. I wrote him a letter almost every day. Boxing matches, photographs. Just something for him to open up. He never wrote back to me once.

But he did call me one morning when I was ready to go to work. I said, 'Mike! Oh man, how are you?' And he said, 'I just wanted to thank you. It's really helped me.' I said, 'Mike, you're my brother. I love you.' And he said, 'Well, I just wanted to say thanks.' But on the visit we just talked about handball, which he knew all about because of Jim and me and also I think he'd been playing with these guys. And we talked about the doorman in my apartment building. What was happening in New York City. For forty-five minutes, an hour, just to say hello, to see him. It was great to see him, you know?

And then he married again, and that was good for him for a time. For a time. Dr Monica Turner. And had another kid. And it played real well with the press. 'Cause Monica seemed Miss Goody-Two-Shoes in their eyes. A doctor. Someone to put him right, right? Except she wasn't really like that. In reality she was different.

KEVIN ROONEY: He lost all focus. He lost the three main guys, who were Cus, Jimmy and Bill. I mean, that wasn't his fault, to be honest, and he was never really close to Bill. But he lost Steve Lott, who was his friend. He lost me. Cus put everyone into place and he walked away from all of us. And Cus tells Jimmy, when he knows he's dying, he says, 'Jimmy, make sure Mike doesn't end up broke.' So then Jimmy and Bill took out this insurance policy that Mike was going to get $250,000 tax free for the rest of his life, and he had to turn that in. That's a fact. And Monica Turner was no goody-two-shoes. She got a couple of million. She's set.

NADIA HUJTYN: To give you an example. At Camille's funeral, because she passed away a couple of years ago, and the new wife was there, if that's what you want to call her. Lowlife. Stereotypical. Worried about her jewellery. Very lowlife. Much lower than I even thought. And she says, 'Guess where he had to sleep?' And I said, 'The couch?' And she said, 'Yup, he had to sleep on the couch.'

August 19, 1995
W DQ R1 vs Peter McNeeley, Las Vegas, NV

December 16, 1995
W KO R3 vs Buster Mathis Jnr, Philadelphia, PA

March 16, 1996
W TKO R3 vs Frank Bruno, Las Vegas, NV
Regains WBC heavyweight title

September 7, 1996
W TKO R1 vs Bruce Seldon, Las Vegas, NV
Regains WBA heavyweight title

Amazingly, he seemed to be getting intimidatory powers back. He didn't want to be doing it any more, really, but he was still scaring the hell out of these guys. McNeeley was a joke, and the trainer threw the towel in after approximately thirty seconds, at least that's what it seemed. But actually McNeeley had had a go for a few seconds, and that had thrown him off stride very momentarily at the start. But the problem for McNeeley was he was a complete no-hoper. A total, almost embarrassing tomato can, and even on McNeeley's very best night and Mike's very worst one, McNeeley wouldn't have a prayer with him. But it showed him that he was rusty, and he'd have to get in shape more. But it wasn't a big problem. It was a one-rounder, for Chrissakes. And it was always gonna be. Then they gave him Mathis, who was never going to be up to it and was a curious type of guy who seemed to box only because his old man had boxed, and really wasn't very good. So that was easy.

And then Don gave him Bruno again for a version of the title, and that was so easy, because Bruno didn't put up a fight this time. At all. Bruno crossing himself about fifty times just walking to the ring. So it was over before it started, basically. He was surprised by that. Maybe Bruno had gone a little crazy. He was certainly acting oddly. Probably he remembered the last time – the pain he had inflicted on him. Well, it was all about money, wasn't it? And somewhere in that dressing room Bruno had lost his nerve. If only Bruno had known how fragile his own confidence was. That was what was odd. 'Cause normally fighters notice things like that. Any weakness. But the problem with him and Bruno was they'd been through the mill for too many years. But he was still putting up a good act. And then they gave him Seldon for another version of the title and Seldon was shitting himself, he was so intimidated. Seldon didn't even try to fight. He laid down when he hadn't even caught him with a proper punch. So he was just beating people with his aura again, which he didn't think he'd get back. Well, long may it continue! If only they knew! And then there was the Holyfield fight coming up, and that was just huge money, and it would be easy, and maybe after that he should just retire.

JAY BRIGHT: Mike still had the power, the speed. He had all the attributes – he still has – but I don't think he had the desire any more, and that's a very important piece of the puzzle.

November 9, 1996
   L TKO R11 vs Evander Holyfield, Las Vegas, NV
   Loses titles

June 28, 1997
   L DQ R3 vs Evander Holyfield, Las Vegas, NV

Holyfield, very much the underdog, shows no sign of being intimidated despite his smaller build and Tyson's reputation, and hands Tyson a beating for much of the fight. However, such is the money generated that a quick rematch is arranged. This time, what occurs is sensational. Tyson, again behind, bites Holyfield on both ears, forcing the referee, Mills Lane, to call a halt. A riot ensues at the MGM Grand casino.

KEVIN ROONEY: If the referee hadn't stopped it in the first Holyfield fight, Mike would've been knocked cold. Mike was all staggering and the referee jumped in. Then they had the rematch and he got in better shape.

TEDDY ATLAS: With Holyfield, he became a game quitter. He stopped trying to win. And the second time against Holyfield he knew he would actually have to be a fighter. And I said beforehand, two nights before the fight – I said he was going to have to foul to get out of the fight. I was sitting here trying to figure it out and then, bingo! He's setting his alibi up. He could headbutt, hit low or bite. I watched the fight at a party at the house of Jack Newfield [the late investigative journalist]. Tyson goes out and throws a bomb, a desperation punch. Holyfield is having none of the silent agreement. Then he bit him! I was so frustrated, because I only had my wife with me when I said it. So you see Tyson was a fractured, scared, incomplete person who could not face a man. He would not have entered that room against Holyfield again if he didn't know where the door was. He was planning it two days before. That's what made me realise.

But what people didn't realise was how dirty Holyfield was with his head. Obviously, a fight is a fight, when it comes down to it, it's not just 'sport', it's different, but there are still limits, A head is harder even than a punch. And Holyfield used it all the time. Every time they went into a clinch. The referee did nothing. But, yeah, he lost his own head completely. What he did was... indescribable. But Holyfield making out he was this man of Christ and then coming in with these persistently illegal tactics – it was too much, man. You can only take so much. And Holyfield cut him as well, and maybe he was just off-form anyway. Maybe he shouldn't be doing it any more. But he didn't have the money he thought he had, and probably he'd spent far too much. Far too much. So maybe he should go abroad and get some easy paydays. Like Jack Johnson did. Yeah, like Johnson. And there was always Lewis. That would be a big pot of gold. Real big. And Jesus, he needed it.

NADIA HUJTYN: He wasn't smart with any of it [the money]. And there were ex-wives, and children – the first one's name was D'Amato. And he's got to pay for all these children. I wouldn't know if he stays in touch with them. I know he liked the last two, and he brought them to Camille's house on occasion. He used to make comments that he ought to do better things because he's got these children, but it doesn't last longer than saying it, unfortunately.

KEVIN ROONEY: He's trying to make out he's a family man and I'm sure he does love his kids but he ain't no family man. He likes fooling around with girls.

STEVE LOTT: And when the therapists examined him, he just said he was a bad kid and always had been. And when they said, 'Well, we want to find out why that is,' Mike didn't have the balls to tell them the truth – that he'd been a hero, and been happy. None of the therapists knew that Mike had been with Jacobs, Cayton and us. None of them called me. None of them tried to find out what Mike was like with us. They called him in and said, 'Tell us about yourself.'

And he said, 'Well, I'm a bad kid from Brooklyn. I've been in reform schools all my life.' So the therapists say, 'Mike, let's address that.' You see, Mike couldn't tell the doctors the truth. He couldn't say, 'Listen, I'm a very sad kid. Why? Because I was a hero and I had all these wonderful people around me. And then along came Don King and Robin Givens and I fell for their acts. I loved Cus but then I fell for their scams.'

January 16, 1999
  W KO R5 vs Francois Botha, Las Vegas, NV

October 23, 1999
  NC R1 vs Orlin Norris, Las Vegas, NV

January 29, 2000
  W TKO R2 vs Julius Francis, Manchester, England

June 24, 2000
  W TKO R1 vs Lou Savarese, Glasgow, Scotland

October 20, 2000
  NC R3 vs Andrew Golota, Auburn Hills, MI

October 13, 2001
  W RTD R6 vs Brian Nielsen, Copenhagen, Denmark

So, yeah, he'd gone on the road, to Europe. And it was cool. It was respite. He fought this guy in England,

Francis. He was totally out of his depth. They never really should have put him in there. And Francis knew it. But funnily enough he seemed like a nice guy, and he was game as well. Mike was amazed that he came out for the second. And then he went to Glasgow, Lou Savarese, the Great White Hope. Except he knew he couldn't fight as well. Savarese's whole career was a Primo Carnera act. But you get the winning record and then ultimately you get the money. You've got to lose to get it, and take a beating, depending on how game you are, but as long as you don't get too badly hurt, or get a blood clot on the brain or something, you still get the money, and then you're set. But he did slightly lose the plot against Savarese. He didn't like him. And he was going in to finish it in the first and then the referee stepped in when he wasn't expecting it, 'cause he really wanted to do damage to Savarese, and he got tangled up with the referee, maybe even glanced him with a blow by mistake, and possibly he was lucky not to get disqualified.

But he liked Britain. They really loved him there. It was so different from the States. He went to Brixton, the black area, and they literally had to stop the traffic. And the British cops – the cops! – took him in the police station, and there was this huge crowd down below, and he was on this balcony and he had to address them through this megaphone. It was just surreal. And then he went to Denmark to fight Nielsen, another white who couldn't really fight, but who had this winning record. Something like 60 and 2.

And they really loved him there as well. Nielsen was game, even though he couldn't fight and had this built-up record. You've got to give it to the promoters to make that effort to prepare these guys for the payday. Years, it must take. But it took him longer to finish Nielsen – the sixth – because maybe he wasn't quite in shape, but how do you get motivated to get in shape for these guys? But for Lewis, he would get in shape. Definitely.

JOSÉ TORRES: It is very strange that a person with no control could ever have become champion of the world.

FRANK MALONEY: They didn't even have Francis on the posters. Tyson could've been fighting Mickey Mouse and it would still have sold out. He'd just fought Botha. We sold the fight on the pretence that Julius had a chance of beating Tyson. Even on Tyson's worst night, he beats Julius. One night I'm sitting with Julius's trainer, who was then Mark Roe, and I hear him say, 'And when we beat Tyson...' And I said, 'Mark, you really think Julius has a chance of beating Tyson?' And he goes, 'Well, you do, Frank, the things you've been saying.' So I said, 'Mark, it's my job to hype the fight.' But Julius got a great payday. I saw it as a payday for a man who had served boxing well.

When we get to the weigh-in Tyson is sitting there twirling his hair between his finger and thumb like a lost little girl. He wasn't paying any attention. He was very friendly in the build-up to the fight. And Julius was in awe of him. I could not believe it when Julius went up to him and said, 'Excuse me, Mike, can I have your autograph, please?' This was at the press conference. I mean, I didn't say anything because this was a big day for Julius. But I could not believe it. He was totally in awe of Tyson, and I knew then that we had absolutely no chance of winning this fight, even though I knew that already.

June 8, 2002
L KO R8 vs Lennox Lewis, Memphis, TN
Competing for Lewis's WBC and IBF titles

The Lewis fight is dogged by controversy. At a pre-fight press conference Lewis throws a punch and in the melee that follows Tyson bites Lewis's leg. Tyson is called before the Nevada Athletic Commission to prove his mental fitness to continue boxing. In the fight itself Tyson receives a bad beating and is finally knocked out by a Lewis right hand.

Lewis was just too big. And he could fight. Man, he was a big motherfucker, The best big fucker he'd fought. Fast and accurate and just as awkward as he'd thought, except more so. And just too big. He'd told the corner that early on: 'He's just too big.' Jesus, where was Cus? Lewis would always have been awkward and big but in the old days he would have knocked him out, surely. And Lewis's fists were like rocks. He wasn't remotely intimidated, although he could tell Lewis was nervous in the first, and he had a short chance then. But somehow he knew Lewis would regroup himself mentally as soon as the second. He was pretty tough mentally after that. Damn, he couldn't intimidate him. But he'd known that at the press conference. And also it was emerging that Don and Rory and John had been ripping him off all these years. Even Rory! And he was starting a lawsuit against them. And Monica had left him. She said he was too much. Fucking bitch. And Lewis caught him with this humungous right hand at the end, and he hoped he hadn't got brain damage. But he had been game. He knew from the second that Lewis was going to knock him out. The funny thing was, he felt like hugging Lewis in there, and saying, 'Listen, man, let's just chill out instead of fighting each other.' But when all the shit was said and done, he took his beating like a man.

KEVIN ROONEY: The Tyson I had would have beat Douglas, Holyfield, Lewis. He would've beat all of them. Tyson's losses are when he's in never-never land. I think he would have beaten Muhammad Ali in his prime. That would have been a hell of a fight. I believe he would have knocked out Jack Dempsey. I believe he would have knocked out Rocky Marciano. In my opinion he just laid down against Lewis.

FRANK MALONEY: Before the fight I wanted Lennox to get beat because of the bitchiness in me after the fallout with the new Lewis team. That fight would have been my pension. I didn't make any money at all out of that fight. And I was sitting there looking at Tyson getting ready in his dressing room on the TV monitor and the crazy antics – smashing the wall, like a mad raging bull again, and then I looked at Lewis getting ready, and I went, 'You know what? I would put my house on Lennox Lewis winning this fight.'

JOSÉ TORRES: Tyson never got over Cus's death, because Cus was a father to him.

February 22, 2003
W KO R1 vs Clifford Etienne, Memphis, TN

And then there was this guy Clifford Etienne, but Etienne was nothing. One round. He basically laid down and took the money, like Spinks had. That was fine by him. An easy night's work. And Etienne had been really intimidated, but who really gave a fuck about all that any more. He didn't. He was basically trying to fight as little as possible. But the debts... the debts! He read somewhere he was supposed to have grossed $400 million in his whole career. Well, he never saw nothing like that, that was for sure. Those guys robbed him real good. He saw Don in the street and kicked him, hard. Good. What an idiot he must have been to trust Don. But that was Cus's fault, with his thing about money. And now he owed something like $35 million to the IRS. How do you figure that? And that was after he sold all the houses and everything.

He even had to sell the pet tiger and move down to Phoenix and live in like this ordinary house, and take his own trash out. Iron Mike Tyson, come to this! Plus he was taking all these antidepressants. Robin started that whole manic-depressive shit. But now he couldn't do without them, the drugs. Plus the cocaine, more than he should. Rory started him on that. Well, maybe not Rory per se but Rory knew that scene. And he'd been back to jail because of some fucking motorist, violation of parole et cetera et cetera. But like he said, he quite enjoyed it. He was an institutionalised person because of his early years. Not as bad as some he'd known. He knew of people who'd tried to break back into jail. 'Cause you're safe in there, as long as you can handle yourself, and you don't have to worry about money or where your next meal is coming from. But now he preferred it down in Phoenix. They left you alone there. And most people seemed to like him. In New York, they hated him – the white sportswriters, all white New York people, basically. That fucking rapist, that animal. So now he just told the writers what they wanted to hear. Ogre. The Apeman. Like before the Lewis fight, when he said he'd eat Lewis's children. But people misunderstood that remark. It was just jail trash talk, 'cause of

the rumours about Lewis being gay. So he was telling
Lewis, like, where are your children?

KEVIN ROONEY: Tyson blames everybody else. But
if you really think about it, 'It ain't my fault, it's your
fault. Why don't you step up and admit it?' He could
have earned fifty, a hundred million bucks for a fight,
but he missed that point. King, Horne and Holloway
fucked the money out of Tyson, and all he had to do
was resist them.

NADIA HUJTYN: Mike is very susceptible to
substance abuse. He was going to come and see me at
the gym one day but the guys he was with said 'No'.

STEVE LOTT: Then when he got out, in about '99
when he was still in Vegas, I went to visit him there,
to pitch him about coming back. He called me out of
the blue. I'd never pitched him about coming back
and I thought I'd take a shot. So I called him and said
I was coming out there next week to see my uncle,
who lives in Vegas, and could I stop by and see you?
He said, 'Sure, stop by.' I picked up every picture I
had of him and us from the good days – every fight,
every press conference, a stack like that, to get his
mind back. So I show up at the house and show him
the photographs and they were wonderful. I was there
for an hour, and he had very strange people in the
house. The guy who fixed the gloves, Panama Lewis,
was there.

Carlos 'Panama' Lewis is a sinister figure, a former Don King employee who is permanently banned from any involvement in boxing in the United States. In 1983 he removed the stuffing from the gloves of a fighter he trained, Luis Resto, before Resto's fight with a young prospect called Billy Collins Jr. Over ten rounds Collins suffered horrific facial injuries. He never fought again, became an alcoholic and crashed his car fatally in what was thought to be a successful suicide attempt. Despite the shared association with Lewis, Tyson fires Don King, Rory Holloway and John Horne, alleging that they have embezzled tens of millions of his fight purses. The case is settled out of court. Tyson then hooks up with Shelly Finkel, a veteran New York fight manager.

STEVE LOTT: I said, 'Mike, can I talk to you for a few minutes alone?' This is when Mike had already left King and was with Shelly Finkel. He said, 'Sure.' And he closes the door. I said, 'Mike, I want to talk to you about something that's possible. You can be a hero again. You can be happy again. Come back with your friends. Give it a shot.' He said, 'Steve, I really loved you guys.' I said, 'The reason you don't like being in the public eye is because people laugh at you and call you names. Remember how it was in '85, '86, when you were a hero and doing commercials on TV. You liked being in the public eye then. He said, 'Yeah, you're right.'

So I knew I had to keep going. I said 'Mike, here's what we'll do. Press conferences A, B and C – a whole plan.' He says, 'Steve, that's great, man.' I said, 'I'll be back tomorrow and we'll talk some more about this, OK?' 'Great,' he says. Next morning, I get up for breakfast with a friend – this is how scary it is around Mike – and I have my cellphone on me, which I never usually carry and I never get calls. But I get this call, and as soon as I pick it up I know who it is. 'Hi, Shelly.' So I know what happened. Someone in the house picked up the phone and called Shelly to tell him Steve Lott was out here in Mike's room talking to him. In one moment I know the whole picture of what's around Mike.

Shelly says, 'Steve, you're in Vegas. What're you doing there?' I said, 'I'm talking to Mike.' He says, 'What're you talking about?' So I said, 'I'm talking about him coming back to Bill, Kevin and I.' And he goes, 'No, I have a contract.' I said, 'Shelly, it has nothing to do with you. Let's do what's best for Mike.' 'No! No! No! I have a contract!' I said, 'Shelly, contracts are easy. We can work that out.'

That day I go back to Mike. I say, 'Mike, something weird happened to me this morning. I got a call from Shelly. Did you call him about me?' 'No.' So it was somebody in the house, the same way that Don always had someone around reporting back on him. As bad as Don was with Mike, at least with Don, Mike was getting big fights.

KEVIN ROONEY: I think that everything that Mike has to say after the Spinks fight is total bullshit.

Anything that King has had to say is total bullshit. Tyson was playing the game, pointing fingers at people. Stupid. Shut up, accept it, and be a man about it.

Part Four

THE END

July 30, 2004
  L KO R4 vs Danny Williams, Louisville, KY

June 11, 2005
  L TKO R6 vs Kevin McBride, Washington, DC

He did get in shape for Danny Williams, down in Phoenix with Jeff Fenech. Well, Jeff didn't think he got in shape enough but he knew that by his recent standards he had. Jeff was a good guy, a real tough guy. He had been a real throwback fighter. Featherweight champion, almost in the mould of the real savage old-time fighters like Battling Nelson. And Williams surprised him. He was this big goofy guy and he thought he was intimidated but obviously he wasn't. Or maybe he just marshalled his fear, like Cus always said. But he thought he was just going to be another average British guy, another Julius Francis. And then he twisted his knee in the early rounds, and couldn't get no leverage with his hooks. But he had to give it to Williams. He could fight a little bit. Of course, in the old days he would have taken him out in one, two rounds. He was about the Alex Stewart level of ability. But Williams did stand up to him when he was really clipping him with some shots in the first two rounds, and then he came on strong. And when Williams was coming on strong he just thought, 'I don't need this any more. I'm through.' He wasn't knocked out or nothing. He'd just had enough. Williams did catch him with this kind of onslaught, but it wasn't enough to knock him out. It wasn't like Douglas. He just went down. And that was it. But Shelly did a good job playing up the knee angle, which was actually true, and the American writers generally bought it but the British writers were just crowing, as you might expect. It was kind of like they'd had enough of him. In fact it was kind of like everybody had had enough of him. It was unbelievable, actually. And the debts, the debts...

The Kevin McBride fight he didn't really want, but they paid him a couple of million so he had to, and McBride was supposed to be this total tomato can who'd lost to anyone even remotely good. So it would be one round, right? But he really didn't get in shape for that one. Jeff knew it but it was too late by the time he showed up in camp to do anything about it. And McBride was better than they'd said. He was another of these big motherfuckers and he just kept leaning down on his shoulders, down on him with this fucking great Irish bulk, tiring him out. And the referee wasn't doing nothing about it, so he did a few things back. That's what people don't understand: you've got to, when you're smaller. 'Defend yourself at all times,' you know? And if someone is being dirty with you, you defend yourself back in the same way. He was still ahead on points but then McBride started rallying and this time he didn't wait for the onslaught. He just went down from push, and he was lying there, praying that the referee would stop it, but it was the end of the round and he just sent him back to the corner instead. But Jeff knew how he was feeling and pulled him out between rounds. And told the press afterwards that he had no heart for this game any more, and that was true. But there was this big black crowd there, fifteen thousand guys from the ghetto wearing alligator shoes and sharp suits, and these real good-looking women all dressed up in their finery, his people, you know? And they booed him from the arena. They booed him...

McBride was indeed 'laying on'. Tyson appeared to become enraged, aiming numerous low blows at his opponent and at one point trying to break his arm in a clinch, just as he had done with Francois Botha.

KEVIN ROONEY: He just laid down again in the McBride fight when he was ahead on the scorecards. If I'm in his corner, 'Hey, Mike, you wanna quit? You're ahead. What's the matter with you?' The Mike

Tyson that I had would never have done that. He quit like a pig. He took the money and ran.

TEDDY ATLAS: The last two fights were just more of him being exposed. They were just ordinary kids. The Irish kid was the more ordinary. He'd fought at a decent level four times and he'd been knocked out four times. Danny Williams, there was a little bit about him, but not that much. People who say Tyson wasn't interested any more piss me off. That's just excusism and ignorance. Tyson doesn't have character. The man's got no substance. If we were talking about astrology, he would be a comet that maybe for a moment was flashing, but its future was always going to be short and inconsequential in the hierarchy that exists in the solar system. He would have his moment as long as he didn't collide with anything bigger.

KEVIN ROONEY: Anything Teddy Atlas tells you is bullshit. I would dismiss it all. He's full of shit.

TEDDY ATLAS: I want to consider myself a niche above Rooney. 'Cause if I'm on an anthill, I think I'm on Mount Everest compared to him. Do you remember that terrible situation down in Guyana years ago with Jim Jones and the poison? All I can tell you is that if Cus had the poison, Rooney would have been first in that line. And if the first ten people had already fallen and you had a chance to refuse it and run away, Rooney would have asked for two cups.

DON MAJESKI: Yeah, Atlas did become mainstream. And I think Rooney is probably a lost cause. But I think he speaks from the heart.

TEDDY ATLAS: Those two last fights said it. As soon as resistance came along, the devil would start knocking at Mike Tyson's door. And he was always like that.

So here he was, it's 10pm in some town in England, and Mike Tyson is doing some bullshit speaking tour. Well, no, it wasn't exactly bullshit, 'cause they were nice people organising it. But it wasn't what he did. What he did was gone, unless he wanted to get brain damage. And he didn't even want to do what he did, for years, so what the fuck was he going to do now? And he was sitting next to Frank Bruno, who apparently had a nervous breakdown or something. And Bruno seemed like some empty shell, totally uncommunicative except when the audience asked him questions, and then he gave this patter that he remembered from their fights. He had more life still in him than Bruno but... what had they done to each other? Really? And Bruno seemed shrunken, somehow. Well, he wished Bruno had been more shrunken when they fought, 'cause he was a big strong bastard then.

So with Bruno not talking, he just sat there drinking

wine, and the waitress who brought him the wine was quite attractive and seemed to be flirting with him, so who knows there? And the audience started asking him questions, and he had to stand up, because he'd agreed to, and all he said was, 'I just hope my ex-wives and children stop asking me for so much money.' Which was probably very inappropriate, but they laughed. And it wasn't exactly the Las Vegas Hilton. It was more like this small club on the outskirts of this town. In the north of England, was it? The tables weren't even full. So then he sat down again, and the waitress brought him another glass of wine and they talked some more. And he looked out at the diners and he knew the journey was over and he'd have to regroup, somehow. Somehow. And sitting there in his suit looking out at the smoky English gloom of the room he saw... nothing.

NADIA HUJTYN: Cus used to say, 'I will have succeeded when he becomes independent of me.' But Mike needed the guidance much longer. I would actually say for ever. Mike never could have looked after himself.

KEVIN ROONEY: Cus was the best.

DON MAJESKI: But, yeah, they really were the lost boys.

TEDDY ATLAS: The truest thing you should get,

and I think it was Budd Schulberg, he was quoted and it was one of the most accurate things anyone had ever said, and I was kind of shaken. He said anyone who stayed with Cus had to be an incomplete individual and never develop a complete personality or an identity for themselves. He said if you look at the history, all the people that formed the group that I'm describing, they wind up having a falling-out with Cus and they leave. The ones that are incomplete in their make-ups, they would be the ones that would become part of the clan, the cult. And Schulberg said that anyone who had their own way of thinking, they might come with Cus when they were young, but if they developed towards normal status, they'd always wind up leaving. They'll all end up leaving the ship, and the others will walk the plank. And when I read it I said, this guy understands Cus. Holy shit! It was like a revelation in a way. It was almost like seeing somebody after you've been on an island by yourself. You finally saw somebody and you were so glad to see somebody else. And you know what: I think the worst quality of Tyson was what he did to people. He would make people howl for their meals. He would make people compromise and lose themselves – just to be in there. He would make a human being howl. He brought the worst out of people. And one after another, Shelly Finkel, other guys before, they've walked down this fucking plank into the sea of lost souls. And the worst thing was Tyson knew he had that power.

KEVIN ROONEY: Teddy Atlas is a fuckin' asshole, trust me. Anything he says is bullshit. If he was in here now I would ignore him.

TEDDY ATLAS: And Cus had this story. When he was a boy, that a monster lived near his school. People believed it. They would walk home a different way to avoid it, even though going past where the monster lived was the quickest way. Then one day Cus is late and he knows he's going to get a beating from his father so he goes the quick way. He's scared. He's shaking. He turns the corner. As he does so he sees the first claw. Then he sees the second claw. And there it is. An old tree. Nothing but an old tree swinging in the wind. And it's ironic that Tyson was just the tree in the end. Cus's guy ended up being the tree.

FRANK MALONEY: I don't think Tyson's a sympathetic character. I don't know what to make of him. A man who's earned all that money and lost it all – you can't feel sorry for him. He's either got to be mentally disturbed or he just doesn't put any value on anything.

DON MAJESKI: All D'Amato's boys wound up broke or in debt so maybe money did mean nothing to them. That unconscious thing he put in their heads. Money is just something you use when you have it.

JAY BRIGHT: I hope he's OK. I haven't really spoken to him lately. You never know where he is. He travels like you breathe. I don't think he's running away from anything. But I hope he's happy.

NADIA HUJTYN: To me, Mike will always be a hurt child. That's what he is. He never wanted the responsibility of being champion of the world. He never wanted to be a role model. He's crying out, and he always was.

JOSÉ TORRES: Now I feel sorry for Tyson. He called me a few times four or five months ago. I spoke to him. I don't want to get involved with him but I feel sorry for him. I don't want to get involved with him because he can bring trouble. But if I can help him, I will help him. That I will do.

And he got the girl! This 'northern lass', as she called herself. Northern lass! He liked that. And maybe at the next 'speaking engagement' the audience got a little pissed off that he was speaking to her so much, and not speaking to them, and maybe he shouldn't have done that, but he needed it, you see. And you've gotta travel, man, see the world! And also the way they were, the audience, kind of dour, slightly surly by the end, was probably because he was black and she was white and he brought her along. That was what was behind it. Like Jack Johnson! All these fucking years later. And that happens all the time. Yes, the affection. It wasn't even really the sex, although you gotta perform, mumma. He needed the affection. He needed it... he needed it...

KEVIN ROONEY: Basically, he's a good kid.

Acknowledgements

Susie Hilton Knox, Jonathan Rendall's former wife and the mother of his three children, came across this manuscript among his belongings. When approached about possible publication, Rebecca Nicolson and Aurea Carpenter of Short Books were immediately responsive. Gervase de Wilde provided legal advice. But the person probably most deserving of acknowledgement is Mark Stanton, who, as Jonathan's agent during the time he was researching and writing the drafts of *Scream*, negotiated the deal with the original publisher and tried to bring it to fruition. The editor would like to dedicate this edition to George, Sofia and Xanthe Rendall.

– Richard Williams

Tyson's Professional Boxing Record

March 6, 1985
  W TKO R1 vs Hector Mercedes, Albany, NY
  Professional debut

April 10, 1985
  W TKO R1 vs Trent Singleton, Albany, NY

May 23, 1985
  W KO R4 vs Don Halpin, Albany, NY

June 20, 1985
  W TKO R1 vs Ricardo Spain, Atlantic City, NJ

July 11, 1985
  W TKO R2 vs John Alderson, Atlantic City, NJ

July 19, 1985
  W KO R3 vs Larry Sims, Poughkeepsie, NY

August 15, 1985
W KO R1 vs Lorenzo Canady, Atlantic City, NJ

September 5, 1985
W KO R1 vs Michael Johnson, Atlantic City, NJ

October 9, 1985
W TKO R1 vs Donnie Long, Atlantic City, NJ

October 25, 1985
W KO R1 vs Robert Colay, Atlantic City, NJ

November 1, 1985
W TKO R1 vs Sterling Benjamin, Latham, NY

November 13, 1985
W KO R1 vs Eddie Richardson, Houston, TX

November 22, 1985
W TKO R2 vs Conroy Nelson, Latham, NY

December 6, 1985
W TKO R1 vs Sammy Scaff, New York, NY

December 27, 1985
W TKO R1 vs Mark Young, Latham, NY

January 11, 1986
W TKO R1 vs David Jaco, Albany, NY

January 24, 1986
W TKO R5 vs Mike Jameson, Atlantic City, NJ

February 16, 1986
W TKO R6 vs Jesse Ferguson, Troy, NY

March 10, 1986
  W KO R3 vs Steve Zouski, Uniondale, NY

May 3, 1986
  W Decision vs James Tillis, Glens Falls, NY

May 20, 1986
  W Decision vs Mitch Green, New York, NY

June 13, 1986
  W TKO R1 vs Reggie Gross, New York, NY

June 28, 1986
  W KO R1 vs William Hosea, Troy, NY

July 11, 1986
  W KO R2 vs Lorenzo Boyd, Swan Lake, NY

July 26, 1986
  W KO R1 vs Marvis Frazier, Glens Falls, NY

August 17, 1986
  W TKO R10 vs Jose Ribalta, Atlantic City, NJ

September 6, 1986
  W TKO R2 vs Alfonso Ratliff, Las Vegas, NV

November 22, 1986
  W TKO R2 vs Trevor Berbick, Las Vegas, NV
  Wins WBC heavyweight title

March 7, 1987
  W Decision vs James Smith, Las Vegas, NV
  Wins WBA heavyweight title

May 30, 1987
  W TKO R6 vs Pinklon Thomas, Las Vegas, NV
  Retains WBC and WBA titles

August 1, 1987
  W Decision vs Tony Tucker, Las Vegas, NV
  Wins IBF belt and unifies heavyweight division

October 16, 1987
  W TKO R7 vs Tyrell Biggs, Atlantic City, NJ
  Retains all titles

January 22, 1988
  W TKO R4 vs Larry Holmes, Atlantic City, NJ
  Retains all titles

March 21, 1988
  W TKO R2 vs Tony Tubbs, Tokyo, Japan
  Retains all titles

June 27, 1988
  W KO R1 vs Michael Spinks, Atlantic City, NJ
  Retains all titles

February 25, 1989
  W TKO R5 vs Frank Bruno, Las Vegas, NV
  Retains all titles

July 21, 1989
  W TKO R1 vs Carl Williams, Atlantic City, NJ
  Retains all titles

February 11, 1990
L KO R10 vs James 'Buster' Douglas, Tokyo, Japan
Defeated for first time and loses all titles

June 16, 1990
W KO R1 vs Henry Tillman, Las Vegas, NV

December 8, 1990
W TKO R1 vs Alex Stewart, Atlantic City, NJ

March 18, 1991
W TKO R7 vs Donovan Ruddock, Las Vegas, NV

June 28, 1991
W Decision vs Donovan Ruddock, Las Vegas, NV

August 19, 1995
W DQ R1 vs Peter McNeeley, Las Vegas, NV

December 16, 1995
W KO R3 vs Buster Mathis Jr, Philadelphia, PA

March 16, 1996
W TKO R3 vs Frank Bruno, Las Vegas, NV
Regains WBC heavyweight title

September 7, 1996
W TKO R1 vs Bruce Seldon, Las Vegas, NV
Regains WBA heavyweight title

November 9, 1996
L TKO R11 vs Evander Holyfield, Las Vegas, NV
Loses titles

June 28, 1997
  L DQ R3 vs Evander Holyfield, Las Vegas, NV

January 16, 1999
  W KO R5 vs Francois Botha, Las Vegas, NV

October 23, 1999
  NC R1 vs Orlin Norris, Las Vegas, NV

January 29, 2000
  W TKO R2 vs Julius Francis, Manchester, England

June 24, 2000
  W TKO R1 vs Lou Savarese, Glasgow, Scotland

October 20, 2000
  NC R3 vs Andrew Golota, Auburn Hills, MI

October 13, 2001
  W RTD R6 vs Brian Nielsen, Copenhagen, Denmark

June 8, 2002
  L KO R8 vs Lennox Lewis, Memphis, TN
  Competing for Lewis's WBC and IBF titles

February 22, 2003
  W KO R1 vs Clifford Etienne, Memphis, TN

July 30, 2004
  L KO R4 vs Danny Williams, Louisville, KY

June 11, 2005
  L TKO R6 vs Kevin McBride, Washington, DC

Index